W9-AGB-538

DARKROOM BASICS

... and beyond

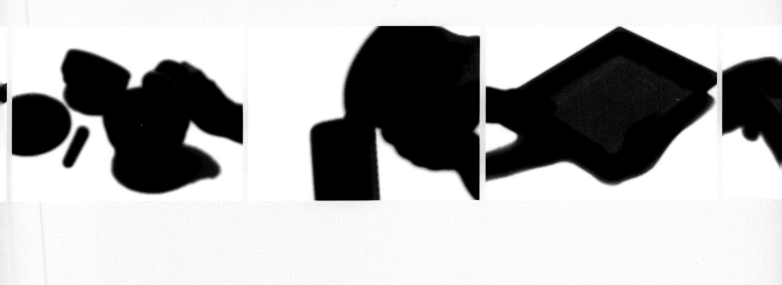

DARKROOM BASICS

... and beyond

ROGER HICKS AND FRANCES SCHULTZ

COLLINS & BROWN

CAUTION

Always handle poisonous and corrosive chemicals with care. Follow the manufacturer's instructions; store chemicals in a secure place, out of the reach of children and in clearly marked, non-food containers. Information, advice and statements made in this book with regard to methods and techniques are believed to be true and accurate. However, neither the author, copyright holder nor publisher can accept legal liability for omissions.

For Jack Cull

First published in Great Britain in 2000 by
Collins & Brown Limited
London House
Great Eastern Wharf
Parkgate Road
London SW11 4NQ

Distributed in the United States and Canada by Sterling Publishing Co.
387 Park Avenue South, New York, NY 10016 USA

Copyright © Collins & Brown Limited 2000
Text copyright © Roger Hicks and Frances Schultz 2000
Please refer to the picture credits on page 128 for photography copyright.

The rights of Roger Hicks and Frances Schultz to be identified as the authors of this work has been asserted by them in accordance with the Copyright, Designs and Patents Act, 1988.

All rights reserved. No part of this publication may be reproduced, stored in a retrieval system, or transmitted in any form or by any means, electronic, mechanical, photocopying, recording or otherwise, without the prior written permission of the copyright owners.

9 8 7 6 5 4 3 2 1

British Library Cataloguing-in-Publication Data:
A catalogue record for this book is available from the British Library.

ISBN 1 85585 812 6

Editorial Director: Sarah Hoggett
Editor: Ian Kearey
Design: Amzie Viladot, Design for Publishing

Reproduction by Classic Scan, Singapore
Printed and bound in Hong Kong by Dai Nippon

This book was typeset using Frutiger and Grotesque.

CONTENTS

INTRODUCTION:

WHY DARKROOM?

Darkroom work is like religion, art or music: if you have to ask what people see in it, you are unlikely to understand the answers that you are given.

It can be an art, of course, or at least a step in an artistic process. It is without question a craft as well, and there is a pleasure in mastering almost any craft: in being able to turn out what would, in the days of the medieval guilds, have been called a 'masterpiece' that demonstrated your skill and earned you the right to be called a master craftsman. And it is a science: some photographers find great intellectual satisfaction in understanding the physics and chemistry behind what they do, and finding better (or at least different) ways of doing it.

It offers you far greater control over the photographic process than you will ever get if you have to rely on other people, but it is wonderfully open-ended. You don't have to understand very much about what you are doing; you certainly don't need to be a great artist, craftsman or scientist, to do it – and do it well – or to enjoy doing it.

More prosaically, darkroom work is a way of saving money. You need to be very rich indeed to be able to hire printers who can deliver the sort of quality that you can quickly learn to achieve for yourself. This is the real surprise: how much you can do to a very high standard, at a remarkably low cost. We hope that this book will show you where you can save money, and where you might be better advised to spend a little more in order to get much better results.

Darkroom work has a long heritage. The first permanent recorded images from nature were probably made in the 1820s, though unfixed images had been made in the 18th century: the process that is still used today was complete, in its essentials, by about 1840. There is a certain fascination in this, but it can have its drawbacks.

Because photography has been around for so long, there are countless excellent books on the subject, some dating well back into the 19th century. Countless excellent photographers, some of whom seem almost as ancient, are equally willing to impart their knowledge to the novice. The beginner can learn an immense amount from both the old books and the old photographers: there is no sense in reinventing the wheel.

On the other hand, modern materials, papers, cameras, lenses and techniques are different from those of the past, and for the most part better. The old books and the old photographers will not necessarily tell you how to get the best out of them. Indeed, they may on occasion point you in the wrong direction, until you fall into the trap of believing that the old ways were, always and invariably, better than anything we have today. They weren't, and aren't, of course.

This is why, on occasion, we may seem to have given the past more weight than it deserves; but we believe, wholeheartedly, that it is as big a mistake to look only to the future, and ignore the past, as it is to look only to the past, and ignore the future. You have to know what to ignore, and when. If you and we, as photographers, have one great advantage over our predecessors, it is this: we have access to most of the best of the past, as well as the best of the present.

These are the good old days.

WORKING LIGHT SYMBOLS

To make life easier, we have used three symbols to show whether you need to work in complete darkness (black bulb) or by safelight (grey bulb), or whether you can work in normal room lighting or daylight (white bulb).

Normal room lighting or daylight

Safelight

Complete darkness

▶ *Size matters*

This is pretty close to a straight print, but for publication we decided to burn in the top a little as the overly light stonework was taking away the emphasis on the sheer crowding and motion of the pigeons. Even 'happy snaps' work better as decent-sized prints (this goes very well to 30 x 40 cm/12 x 16 in for exhibition); and a well-exposed picture deserves a well-made print.

GETTING STARTED

S ooner or later, if you get serious
about darkroom work, you are
going to want somewhere permanent
to work. You are also going to want
all kinds of darkroom goodies. But
everyone has to start somewhere, and
most photographers start with a
temporary set-up in the bathroom,
kitchen, basement, or anywhere else
that can be blacked out. A good guide
to how dark your darkroom needs to
be is this: if you can't see your hand
in front of your face after five
minutes, it's dark enough.

Setting up a darkroom and getting
first-class results is easier than you
think. After that, what you need is
practice, particularly for so-called
'advanced' techniques. Materials are
expensive, but not impossibly so, and
you can learn an immense amount for
the price of a few rolls of film, a
couple of boxes of paper, and the
chemistry you need to process both.

TEMPORARY DARKROOMS

The most usual room for a temporary darkroom is the bathroom. Sooner or later, though, most photographers manage to colonize another room on a dual-use basis. A cloakroom may be remodelled or a guest bedroom may be blacked out; or even the dining room may be used.

Running water is not essential, as mixed chemicals can be brought in, and washing can be done elsewhere. Two things are, however, essential: an electrical supply and a good blackout. In many countries, bathrooms are not permitted to have electrical sockets, because of the risk of electrocution. In such cases, a multi-socket extension lead is the only option. The smaller the darkroom, the more important ventilation becomes. An electric extractor fan in the ceiling may seem expensive, but it is almost certainly worth it. At least, open the door periodically to change the air. In summer, ventilation helps to keep the darkroom cool.

Heating, whether for the whole room or just in the form of tray heaters, is likely to be essential in winter. Developers work very slowly at less than about 18°C/65°F, quite apart from the discomfort.

Blacking out

Blackout fabric, available from curtain shops, is effective, cheap and easy to find. An oversize piece, wedged in a window with battens, is quick and

 ## setting up a temporary darkroom

This removable darkroom is installed in a small toilet: the whole room is no more than 160 cm (63 in) deep and around 75 cm (30 in) wide. The upper level is the 'dry side' for the enlarger, paper, and so on. The lower level is the 'wet side', a 51 x 61-cm (20 x 24-in) tray resting on the toilet pan.

A step-stool allows access to the enlarger, and allows prints to be processed comfortably while sitting down. The safelight (not visible in these photographs) is over the door, and both it and the enlarger run off an extension socket run in from outside.

Ventilation is via a ceiling-mounted extractor fan (not visible in these photographs) that runs only when the main light is switched on, and for five minutes afterwards; this is obviously as much use in a WC as in a darkroom. There is no heating, as body heat keeps the room warm even in winter. A tray heater would be useful at the beginning of winter sessions, to keep the chemicals warm.

The actual blackout takes under one minute to install; the work table another 30 seconds; and the whole darkroom, as illustrated, under 10 minutes – see page opposite for blacking out the door.

Incidentally, the pictures below are not distorted. The top of the door really does slant like that, and the wall on the right is curved. Victorian craftmanship was not always what it was cracked up to be!

1 Clear out everything not fixed in the room, including – usually – the toilet paper: it is all too easy to splash it. This takes one or two minutes.

2 Black out the window, first with thin plywood, then with blackout fabric wedged in place with battens. This takes under one minute to install.

easy to set up and remove. It can also be secured with velcro, or bought in made-to measure blinds, with side channels (to fit flush with the window frame), for near-instant blackout.

Three ways to black out doors are a curtain of blackout material hung over the door (rolled round a dowel when not in use); 'sausage'-type draught excluders at the bottom of the door; and painting the inside edges of the door and door-frame with blackboard paint.

As long as you cannot see your hand in front of your face after five minutes, a simple blackout should be adequate for printing. But if you want to load film during the day (many darkrooms are suitable for use only at night), you will probably need twin blackouts on the window. In this situation, a piece of plywood is effective but bulky (don't use hardboard or Masonite, as these materials are too flexible); specialist darkroom suppliers sell opaque black film that clings to the glass electrostatically and can be peeled off and used many times.

useful tips

• Although cellars make wonderful darkrooms, they can be cold and damp: as well as fitting a heater, consider a dehumidifier.

• A low-wattage greenhouse heater can be ideal for very small darkrooms.

• An off-cut of vinyl flooring can be used to protect floors.

• Boil a kettle for a few minutes to flood a small room with steam and settle the dust.

NOVA DARKROOM TENT

The Nova Darkroom Tent is about 110 cm (42 in) square and 200 cm (78 in) high, and can be set up anywhere. An air pump inflates the darkroom and changes the air when the door is zipped closed. Power and water can be run in via light-trapped 'trunks'.

All our pictures for publication were printed in this tent for almost a decade, during which time we illustrated books and wrote magazine articles. We used a Nova Tank for processing, but processed prints were dumped into a holding tank (a big beer-cooler box) and periodically taken out for washing in batches.

3 The work surface goes in next, with the enlarger. This is the most demanding part of the set-up. If you don't have a dado rail, as here, use folding legs or a trestle.

4 Four 20 x 25-cm (8 x 10-in) trays sit inside a big 51 x 61-cm (20 x 24-in) tray: developer, short stop, fixer and plain water, the last for use as a holding tank.

PERMANENT DARKROOMS

A permanent darkroom is a wonderful luxury, and the amount of space required to build one may well be less than expected. Of course, if you have a convenient corner in a garage, basement or any other room, you can leave a darkroom tent (see page 11) set up permanently.

Permanent darkrooms have been built in attics, garden sheds and garages, and made by partitioning off other rooms. The time-honoured suggestion of building a darkroom under the stairs may be feasible in large, old houses, though few under-stair spaces are in fact large enough. Even if they have room for a permanent darkroom, most people have to settle for something short of their ultimate desires, so it makes sense to begin with the dream, and then to make such compromises as are dictated by space and money.

The first thing about a darkroom is that it should be divided into a dry side and a wet side. The dry side is for enlargers, paper, film loading and the like. The wet side is for processing and washing. Running water is not absolutely necessary, but if at all possible, there should be two cold taps (one for washing prints or films, one for general use) and one hot.

In a dream darkroom, the entire wet bench will be a shallow sink, or at least, a waterproof worktop with a large sink installed. The dry side may incorporate more than one enlarger, for different film formats or to facilitate such techniques as combination printing (see page 82) and pre-flashing (see page 77).

There must also be as much storage space as possible, for paper, chemicals and processing equipment such as different sizes of tanks and trays. Numerous power sockets permit the use of enlarger(s), enlarger timer(s), processing machine(s), dryer(s) and more. All electrical equipment should be designed for use in a darkroom, or operated by pull-cords for safety. And, of course, forced ventilation should be a very high priority.

The floor should be waterproof and easily cleaned; a mottled pattern disguises stains. At the edges, a beading of silicone sealant will stop spills from getting under the floor covering. If your lights really are safe, light-coloured walls are better than dark-coloured, as they reflect what light there is, though black walls will have the effect of minimizing reflections around the enlargers.

Dry side

The enlargers, from left to right, are a 1960s MPP Micromatic 5 x 7 in with a 1980s De Vere colour head; a Paterson Pro 67 with dual head for variable contrast and colour; and two 6 x 9 cm Meopta Magnifaxes, the first with a variable contrast head, the second with colour. To the extreme right are the Nova Tanks, and the gas fire which is (surprisingly) safe with black-and-white printing paper.

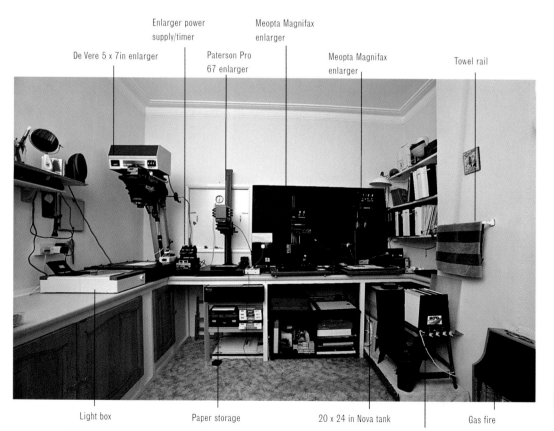

Enlarger power supply/timer

Meopta Magnifax enlarger

De Vere 5 x 7in enlarger

Paterson Pro 67 enlarger

Meopta Magnifax enlarger

Towel rail

Light box

Paper storage

20 x 24 in Nova tank

Gas fire

12 x 16 in Nova tank

Wet and dry sides

If your darkroom is big enough, you can make the dry and wet sides L-shaped. This bench is used for sorting negatives, loading film, and so forth. On the left, there is an RC paper dryer (see page 60); on the right, a light box; and above, a bright 'hot light' with a blue bulb, for judging prints under near-daylight conditions. Even with the big cupboards under here and under the wet side, more storage space would still be useful. There is an air cleaner on the end of the wet bench on the left; these are sold for asthmatics and greatly improve air quality.

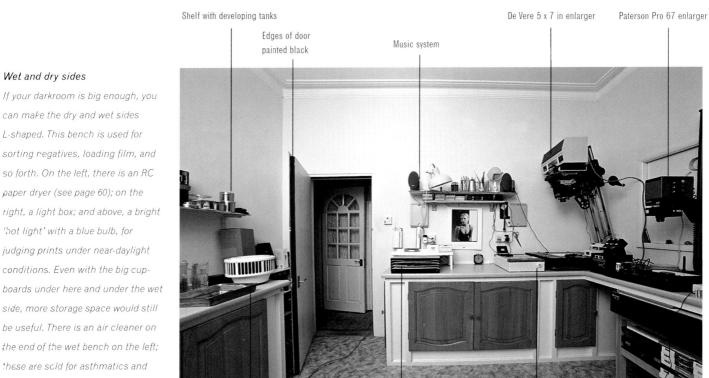

Shelf with developing tanks

Edges of door painted black

Music system

De Vere 5 x 7 in enlarger

Paterson Pro 67 enlarger

Filtaire air cleaner

Nova print dryer

Light box

Wet side

Ideally, this would be rebuilt with a much bigger sink and more taps. In a perfect world, there would have two cold taps, one for the washer and one for general use; one hot tap from the mains supply, for general use; one tempered hot tap, for washing colour; and possibly one distilled water tap as well. The big black thing is a Jobo CPE-2, used for colour processing and for batch-processing 120 and 4 x 5 in black-and-white films. The smaller black object is a (now discontinued) Paterson Orbital processor, used for 5 x 7 in and 8 x 10 in films.

Clock

Storage shelves

MDF 'bung' in window

Shelf with developing tanks

Data sheets taped to back of door

Bookshelf for chemicals

Heater in fireplace

Jobo CPE-2

Paterson Orbital print processor

DARKROOM CHEMISTRY

The made-up solutions used in photography are often called 'chemistry', and we have used this term, despite grammatical objections. There are two essential baths in monochrome photography. In the first of these, the developer 'brings up' the image, converting exposed silver-halide crystals to black, metallic silver. Then the fixer dissolves out the undeveloped silver halide and makes the image permanent. Apart from these, all you need is water for washing.

Although there are a few 'universal' developer formulations, for both paper and film, better results are obtainable from developers formulated for specific purposes: to give a particular image colour on paper ('warm' or 'cool'), to give maximum film speed or the finest possible grain, or whatever.

There is less variation in fixer formulae than among developers, and most are interchangeable. Almost all modern fixers are 'rapid', which simply means that they work faster than the old variety. Although some people still use 'hardening' fixers (see Glossary), there is very rarely any need to do so: films and papers are much tougher than they used to be. Plain 'hypo' fixers, made by dissolving sodium thiosulphate in water, are economical but slow and prone to sludging and other drawbacks unless they are changed very frequently.

LIQUID AND POWDERED CHEMICALS

Powdered chemicals are cheaper than liquid ones, chiefly because there is no water to ship, and last indefinitely until they are 'made up' by being dissolved in water. Although liquid chemicals are more expensive and have a shorter shelf-life, they are vastly more convenient and safer – dissolving powdered chemicals can be tedious, and airborne dust is a health hazard. We recommend liquid chemicals, and have assumed their use throughout.

OTHER CHEMICAL BATHS

As well as the two basic chemical baths – developer and fixer – there are various optional baths for different purposes.

A short stop is a very weak acid bath which is used between the developer and the fixer. It is described more fully on page 36.

Wash aids (see page 59) reduce the wash times for fibre-based paper from 60 minutes or more to 20 minutes or less. Film and resin-coated papers wash fast enough without them.

Wetting agents are used as a final rinse before drying. They are used at very high dilutions (typically 1 part agent to 200 parts water) to encourage the water to run off smoothly, without leaving drying marks.

Toners allow you to change the colour of the silver image and are described at greater length on pages 92 and 94.

FIXING STAGES

It is impossible to see exactly what is going on inside a developing tank, for obvious reasons, but it is possible to get a good idea by stopping at various stages, washing the film well (so that the developer and fixer cease to act) and then opening the tank.

Undeveloped film

Undeveloped film looks much the same whether exposed or unexposed. It darkens slowly on exposure to light, but only very slowly.

Partially-developed film

This Ilford 100 Delta film has been partially developed (90 seconds in Paterson Acutol) and then washed. A weak image can be seen against the creamy silver-halide emulsion after 60 seconds or less. This film was exposed and is now useless.

useful tip

• Buy small glass bottles from a pharmacist, and decant opened bottles of developer stock solution into them. Developer in an opened, half-full plastic bottle may go off in a few days; in a full glass bottle it should keep for weeks.

Fully-developed film

After six minutes the silver image has reached the desired density. Provided you put the film in the fixer immediately, it is possible to turn the room lights on now.

Partially-fixed film

This has been partially fixed in very weak fixer, to show how the unexposed halide begins to dissolve out. Stronger fixer would have worked too fast to get a reliable picture.

Fully-fixed film

Once the film is fully fixed, there is a black silver image against a clear background. Use the manufacturer's recommended fixing time, or the fixer test described on page 36.

DARKROOM HEALTH & SAFETY

Overall, there are three things to remember about safety in the darkroom. The first is that most photographic chemicals are used at very low concentrations, so that even if the ingredients themselves are dangerous, they have been diluted to a point where the risks are considerably lessened. The second is that there are plenty of other everyday chemicals that are at least as dangerous as most photographic chemicals, and often more dangerous: oven cleaner, nail-polish remover, motor fuel and most disinfectants, for a start. The third is that you cannot legislate for common sense: if you need to be told not to drink the developer, or to mistake the developer graduate for a whisky glass, maybe you shouldn't take up photography. Even so:

• Keep all photographic chemicals out of the reach of children, and don't reuse beverage containers.

• Mop up spills as soon as they occur: dried chemicals form dust, which can become airborne and contaminate films, papers, drinks, food – and your lungs.

• Although die-hard photographers have always loved to dabble their fingers in the solutions, a few do end up with painful, irritating rashes as a result of developer poisoning. Surgical gloves or print tongs are a good idea.

▲ *Using extended red film*

This was shot on Ilford SFX, an 'extended red' film with some sensitivity in the near-infrared. Film manufacturers give development times for their own and some rivals' products: developer manufacturers give times for a wider range.

DEVELOPING TANKS

The most basic tool for film development is the developing tank. Almost everyone today uses the 'daylight' type. The film is loaded into them in the dark, of course, but after that, the chemistry can be poured in and out in full daylight. The technique of loading a tank is shown on page 38.

There are basically two kinds of developing tank, plastic and stainless steel. Both consist of an outer shell; a spiral, onto which the film is loaded; a light-trapped lid; and a second, watertight lid that allows the tank to be inverted to agitate the chemicals, even when it is full. Most plastic tanks also have a central core which acts as a light trap: omit this at your peril. Some tanks have removable light traps and gaskets, and a central agitating rod or spindle.

Many people, especially beginners, find plastic tanks easier to use, which is why we have concentrated on them here. It is worth knowing, however, that stainless-steel tanks have some advantages. They are slower to fill and to drain, and loading the film spirals is a knack that can take some learning, but they use less chemistry per film, and the spirals need not be bone-dry when the tank is loaded. Trying to load even a slightly damp plastic spiral is purgatory: it is worth having at least one spare so that you can use a fresh one while another is drying.

Always hold tanks at a slight angle when filling, to reduce the risk of bubbles, especially with plastic reels. Tilt the tank to the same sort of angle as for filling a glass of beer.

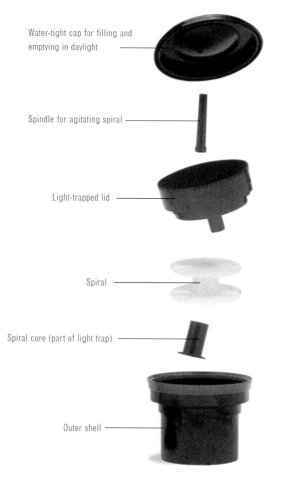

Water-tight cap for filling and emptying in daylight

Spindle for agitating spiral

Light-trapped lid

Spiral

Spiral core (part of light trap)

Outer shell

Water-tight cap for filling and emptying in daylight

Light-trapped lid

Spiral

Outer shell

▲ *Paterson System 4 developing tank*

The Paterson System 4 is typical of plastic developing tanks; this is a single-spiral version. Larger versions are available for multiple spirals, or for 120/220 film; the spirals themselves can be adjusted for both 35mm and 120/220.

▲ *Kinderman stainless-steel tank*

Single-spiral stainless-steel tanks are less common than double-spiral tanks, which take two 35mm spirals or one 120/220. The spirals themselves are not adjustable.

BUY NEW

• Although old developing tanks and spirals are often found at photo fairs, they are rarely worth even the modest prices asked. Buying new is generally a much better idea.

• Even if they are undamaged, tanks may be incomplete —missing a top cap, for instance, or the light-trapping core for the spiral may be missing from plastic tanks.

• Stainless-steel spirals are normally interchangeable between different tanks, and damage is easy to see, but plastic spirals are often incompatible with one another's cores and tanks, and if they have been poorly treated the surface may be roughened and they will be difficult to use.

▼ *Changing bags*

Even if you don't have a really light-tight darkroom, you can still load your films into a developing tank in perfect safety by using a changing bag. These bags range from simple, inexpensive black versions, with elasticated arm-holes, to the elaborate miniature tents used in the movie industry.

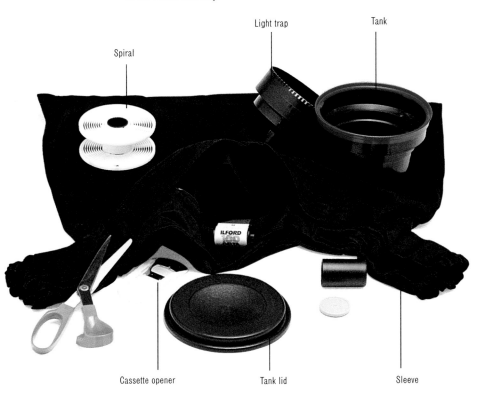

Spiral   Light trap   Tank

Cassette opener   Tank lid   Sleeve

VOLUMES OF CHEMISTRY AND FILL TIMES

Typically, a single-reel plastic developing tank needs 300–450 ml (11–16 fl oz) of developer to process a single 35mm film. A single-reel steel tank rarely needs more than 225 ml (8 fl oz). Double-reel tanks typically take slightly less than twice as much.

A very important point is how fast you can get this developer into and out of the tank – the shorter the development time, the more important it is. A one- or two-reel tank may take 5–25 seconds to fill, and around 10–20 seconds to drain. With a 5-minutes development time, this represents anything from 5–15 per cent of the development time – and a 10 per cent variation can make quite a difference to negative density. To keep variations to a minimum:

• Choose a tank that can be filled and emptied quickly. Four- and six-reel tanks should be treated with caution.

• Practise filling and emptying the tank. A smooth pouring motion can halve the time needed for either operation.

• Be consistent in your timing. You can begin as you start to fill or drain, or as you finish, but don't time from starting to fill to finishing emptying this time, and finishing filling to starting to drain next time.

• Choose longer development times, rather than shorter. Many developers can be used at greater dilutions, to prolong development times.

• If developing times at 24°C (75°F) are inconveniently short, work at 20°C (68°F) – but take care to always use the right time for any given temperature.

VOLUME, TIME AND TEMPERATURE

In order to make up darkroom chemicals to the right strength, you will need several sizes of graduate. At the very least, you will need at least one very small graduate (see below) of 50 ml (2 fl oz) or so, for measuring out concentrated developers and the like, and one medium-to-large graduate of around 1 l (36 fl oz), for measuring the amount you need to fill a developing tray or tank. In practice, it is difficult to get by without at least two medium-to-large graduates, and it is a good idea to have a range of sizes.

TIME AND TEMPERATURE

Prints are developed 'to finality' when all the silver that can be developed, is developed. They can therefore be developed 'by inspection'; in other words, when they look right, they are right.

Film development is another matter entirely. Films are not developed to finality (they would be far too contrasty if they were), and they cannot easily be inspected during development. Each film-and-developer combination has a recommended development time, at a recommended temperature, though these can be varied to suit personal preferences (see page 28), so you must have accurate means of measuring both time and temperature.

Although you can get by with your watch or a wall-clock, provided they have a second hand, purpose-made, dedicated stop-clocks are a lot more accurate for timing.

For reading temperature, most people use spirit thermometers, which are reasonably cheap to buy and accurate enough for black-and-white photography. The spirit column inside the thermometer can, however, fragment, leading to very inaccurate readings.

The most accurate thermometers, as well as being the fastest-responding and most reliable, are mercury-in-glass ones. The most accurate, with 0.2- or even 0.1-degree gradations, have the thinnest mercury thread and are therefore hardest to read. They are ideal as 'reference' thermometers, but they are expensive, and the risk of mercury spillage if the thermometer breaks is one that many do not want to take.

Basic graduate set

A good basic graduate outfit would be one 45 ml (1.8 fl oz); one 300 ml (11 fl oz); a couple of 600 ml (22 fl oz); and a 1200 ml (44 fl oz). Add a big 2 l (72 fl oz) mixing jug, and you are unlikely to have any problems. Purpose-made photographic graduates, like these from Paterson, are more convenient and generally much more accurate than domestic jugs.

Digital stop-clocks

These have the advantages of being inexpensive and easily available. The main disadvantage is that you don't know when the battery may run out, and may spend frantic minutes trying to find a new one.

Mechanical stop-clocks

*Mechanical clocks cost
more than digital ones, but
checking that they are fully
wound becomes almost a
reflex action. Even if the
clock stops while you are
watching, you lose at most a
few seconds as you twist
the key.*

◄ *Dial thermometers*

*Both dial (bimetal, shown here) and
digital thermometers can be very
accurate, but they are not failsafe. It
is essential to check then regularly
against a reference thermometer.*

▲ *Spirit thermometers*

*The cork around the top of this Paterson spirit
thermometer makes it harder to drop, acts as a
buffer if it falls over in a beaker, and stops it
disappearing into a Nova Tank (see page 22).*

(see page 22)

useful tips

• Never use any thermometer as a stirring rod!

• If the column in a spirit thermometer fragments, heat the bulb carefully in hot water until the spirit is at the top of the column, then withdraw it immediately; the column should reunite.

• If the markings on a well-used spirit thermometer are hard to read, run a paint-brush loaded with paint along them, then wipe off immediately with a paper towel. The paint will stay in the grooves and restore legibility.

• The thermometers below were left overnight to equalize; their readings varied by about 0.5°C (1°F) – enough to make a detectable difference in black-and-white and a significant difference in colour. Keep a reference thermometer that you do not normally use: otherwise, if you break your only thermometer and have to replace it, the new may one may not agree with the old one. To keep costs down, use an expensive thermometer for reference and a cheaper replaceable one for use.

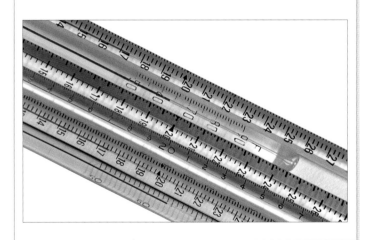

CONSISTENCY AND ACCURACY

In processing, consistency is more important than accuracy. If, for example, your thermometer reads 0.5°C (1°F) low (so that an indicated 20°C/68°F is really 20.5°C/69°F) and you are getting good results with a particular film at a seven minute development time, instead of a recommended eight minute, it doesn't matter as long as you stick to that time and (indicated) temperature. Use a thermometer that reads 0.5°C (1°F) high, so that an indicated 20°C (68°F) is really 19.5°C (67°F), and you will find a detectable difference.

In general, temperature control to plus or minus 0.3°C (0.5°F) is more than adequate; time control to plus or minus 15 seconds will normally be acceptable, except for very short development times (five minutes or under). When measuring volumes, plus or minus two per cent (two in 100 ml or fl oz, or 0.2 in 10) should be reasonably easy to achieve and accurate enough. Working to greater accuracy will do no harm, but it is extremely unlikely to result in any detectable improvement – you can get acceptable results with twice these tolerances.

ENLARGERS AND LENSES

An enlarger is essentially a projector which projects a small image (the negative) onto photographic paper. Old enlargers are often given away, or sold for a song at garage sales. Equally, a state-of-the-art colour enlarger for large negatives (10 x 12.5 cm/4 x 5 in and above) can cost as much as a good new car.

For convenience, we have summarized the requirements of a good enlarger in the panel on the right. One possible heading, 'ease of use', has been omitted because it is arguably better to have a slightly refractory enlarger that delivers good results, rather than one that is easy to use but not very good.

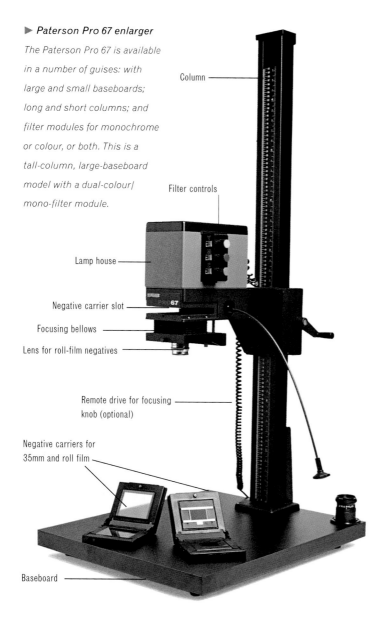

▶ *Paterson Pro 67 enlarger*

The Paterson Pro 67 is available in a number of guises: with large and small baseboards; long and short columns; and filter modules for monochrome or colour, or both. This is a tall-column, large-baseboard model with a dual-colour/ mono-filter module.

Column

Filter controls

Lamp house

Negative carrier slot

Focusing bellows

Lens for roll-film negatives

Remote drive for focusing knob (optional)

Negative carriers for 35mm and roll film

Baseboard

CHECKLIST: WHAT TO LOOK FOR IN AN ENLARGER

Solid construction The best enlargers are built like a railway bridge; only a few are too flimsy to use.

Adequate elevation The enlarger head must travel up far enough to make a decent-sized enlargement: a few don't, and limit you to 20 x 25 cm (8 x 10 in) enlargements, or smaller.

Parallelism The negative holder and the baseboard should be absolutely parallel: of not, you won't be able to hold both sides of the negative in focus at once. Ideally, there should be some way of adjusting parallelism. If there isn't, the enlarger should be sufficiently massive that you will never need to adjust it.

Evenness of illumination The light on the baseboard should be even, without fall-off or 'hot spots'. You can move the bulb up and down to get optimum evenness with many older enlargers. The only way to check evenness is in the dark, either visually or (preferably) with the help of an exposure meter, with no film in the carrier.

Ability to accept filters This is important because most photographers use 'variable-contrast' (VC) papers (see page 52). On some heads you can simply dial in the contrast grade you need; on others, you can dial in colour filtration to control paper contrast; and all but the oldest or cheapest enlargers will either have filter drawers above the lens, or some sort of provision for mounting filters below the lens. Even if you buy an enlarger that cannot accept filters, the Ilford below-lens filter set (see page 52) comes with adapters which normally allow easy use.

Ability to accept a good lens A high-quality lens will give crisper, cleaner pictures with better definition and less distortion, especially in big enlargements. Most lenses and enlargers use the 39 mm x 26 tpi Leica thread: adapters may be available for other sizes.

Most enlargers have a red 'safe' filter that you can swing in under the lens so that you can line up unexposed paper without exposing it. The Paterson shown here is no exception, but the filter is internal, above the lens. For some applications, such as combination printing (page 82), these 'safe' filters are indispensable.

▶ Interchangeable parts

Many older enlargers have interchangeable optical condensers (right): different focal lengths optimize illumination and coverage for different formats. More modern enlargers may have interchangeable mixing boxes (left and centre), again for different formats. A condenser or diffuser for a larger format (6 x 9 cm used with 35 mm, for example) will increase exposure times slightly; a condenser or diffuser for a smaller format (35 mm used on 6 x 9 cm) will almost certainly mean uneven illumination.

Glassless
negative carrier

Glass negative carrier

◀ Negative carriers

The carrier on the right takes negatives up to 6 x 7 cm (2½ x 2¾ in) and has sliding bars to block off unwanted light when using smaller formats or enlarging a part of a bigger negative. The carrier on the left has a mask for 35 mm only and is glassless. Glass carriers hold film flatter (important with larger formats) and prevent 'popping' out of focus as the film heats up in the film gate. Glassless carriers have fewer surfaces to gather dust, and cannot create 'Newton's rings' (below).

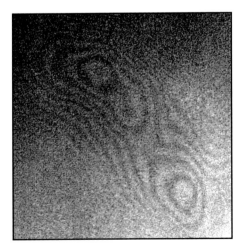

50 mm lens   95 mm lens

◀ Enlarger lenses

Enlarger lenses are sometimes mounted on panels for more rapid interchangeability. These two are a 50 mm for 35 mm negatives. and a 95 mm for roll-film negatives up to 6 x 9 cm (2½ x 2¾ in).

▲ Newton's rings

Newton's rings are interference patterns, formed when two shiny surfaces are pressed together. In a print they look like this, though not usually so obvious: these have been enlarged, and their contrast enhanced, to make them clearer. Often, you are not sure that you are quite seeing them until you realize what they are. They are most obtrusive in skies.

FOCAL LENGTHS FOR ENLARGER LENSES

The focal length of an enlarger lens should be roughly equal to, or greater than, the diagonal of the negative format. Wide-angle enlarging lenses need to be of high quality if they are to be acceptable. A longer focal length will merely reduce maximum enlargement sizes: too short a lens may result in inadequate coverage. Although we have assumed throughout the book that you will be using 35 mm, secondhand enlargers for other formats may be encountered. The normal range of enlarger lenses for the different formats is as follows:

For 35 mm	40–63 mm, with 50 mm as 'standard'
For 645/6 x 6 cm	75–100 mm, with 80 mm as 'standard'
For 6 x 9 cm	90–120 mm, with 105 mm as 'standard'

TRAYS, TANKS AND DRUMS

The traditional way to develop prints – and in the opinion of many, still the best – is in trays. A tray should be slightly bigger than the prints it is intended for, to allow them to be picked up easily. Buy trays in sets, so that you can reserve one for developer, one for short stop, and one for fixer. Many photographers prefer to use the next size up from the print size in use: 25 x 30-cm (10 x 12-in) trays for 20 x 25-cm (8 x 10-in) paper, and so on. Very large trays do, however, occupy a lot of bench space, and take a lot of developer to fill. Buy print tongs, for transferring prints from tray to tray, in colour-coded sets: one pair for developer, one for short stop, and one for fixer. 'Downstream' contamination (developer to short stop to fixer) doesn't matter so much, but dipping the fixer tongs in the developer can drastically shorten developer life, and will mark prints that are picked up with the wrong tongs.

Where space is at a premium, Nova deep-slot tanks are a boon, as they allow even large prints to be processed in remarkably little space:

they are effectively shallow trays, stood on end and sandwiched together. The chemistry can be left ready for use for days or even weeks: set-up and clear-up are reduced to removing and replacing the lids, and wiping up drips – you can pop into the darkroom for 20 minutes and make a print or two. Admittedly, you cannot easily watch the print 'come up', and the tanks are expensive: several times the price of a set of trays. The former should not matter, as if you have got the exposure right you will be developing to finality anyway, and the second is simply a question of budget: if you can afford a Nova tank, it saves a lot of time and space.

Drums are normally used for colour prints, rather than black-and-white ones, but they can be useful, especially for big prints or where space is very limited. The paper is exposed in the darkroom and loaded into the drum, which has a light-trapped cap like a developing tank, so it can be filled and emptied in daylight. Agitation is by 'log-rolling' the drum on a table or even on the floor.

▲ *Set of trays*
Because photographic solutions are normally clear, different-coloured trays, as shown here, are ideal; alternatively, mark them with adhesive labels or indelible markers.

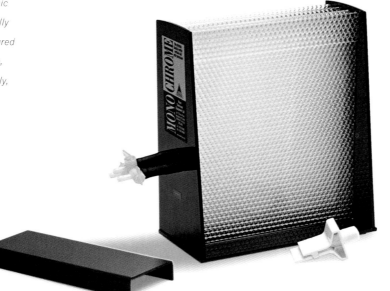

◄ *Nova Monochrome tank*
Nova Monochrome tanks are designed especially for black-and-white printing at room temperature: the 20 x 25-cm (8 x 10-in) model illustrated takes up only 14 x 25 cm (5½ x 10 in) of bench space, though you need room for the drain taps. There is also a larger 30 x 40-cm (12 x 16-in) model.

JUDGING PRINTS DURING DEVELOPMENT

Learning to judge prints while they are developing takes a while. A print like this would look horribly dark by safelight: the temptation would be to 'snatch' it before it is fully developed – in which case, the blacks would be muddy and the wheel would lack 'sparkle'. Always develop prints for the full recommended time, and remember that the only way to judge a print fully is after drying, by the same sort of light under which it will be displayed.

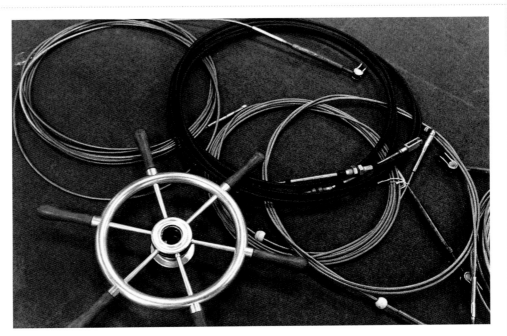

▼ *Nova Quad tank*

More expensive Nova tanks are made in sizes up to 51 x 61 cm (20 x 24 in), and with varying numbers of slots: this is an 20 x 25-cm (8 x 10-in) Quad, with a base that is under 30 cm (12 in) square. All traditional Nova tanks have thermostatically controlled water jackets: process timers with external thermometer probes are optional.

▲ *Drums*

Drums, such as this Durst, are slower to use than trays or Nova tanks, as they have to be washed and dried between each print, but you can do all your test strips (see page 62) in 20 x 25-cm (8 x 10-in) trays or a 20 x 25-cm (8 x 10-in) Nova tank, and then make your exhibition print in the drum. They use surprisingly little chemistry, even for 40 x 51-cm (16 x 20-in) prints.

SAFELIGHTS AND OTHER DARKROOM EQUIPMENT

After graduates, thermometers, timers, film-developing tanks and something in which to develop the prints, the only remaining essential piece of equipment is a safelight: everything else can be improvised, though, as usual, you can buy equipment that will make your life easier.

To test a safelight, rest a couple of coins on a quarter-sheet of paper (there is no sense in using a whole sheet) and leave it as near the safelight as it could normally get, for five times as long as it would normally be left out. Develop it (see page 34), and if there is any shadow of the coins on the paper, either the safelight isn't safe, or there is a light leak somewhere else in the room. For a still better assessment, 'pre-flash' the paper just before the test (see page 77). This will show up even the slightest fogging.

▶ Safelights

The cheapest reliable safelights are the ones with a low-powered bulb (typically 15W) covered by an interchangeable, coloured plastic dome. Most people use orange-brown for monochrome printing, though others prefer to work by traditional red light. In a big darkroom, use two or more safelights.

▼ Portable safelights and torches

A surprisingly useful accessory is a small, portable safelight, which uses an LED: these are from BPS in the United States. If you use a torch (flashlight) in the darkroom, to help you find things, it is a good idea to filter it too. The Mini-Mag illustrated is fully safe at quite short distances if you use both the orange and the red filters together – they are standard Mag-Lite filters, and are supplied with the handy holder – and safe enough for indirect use if you only use one filter or the other.

| useful tip |

• Don't buy any darkroom accessories unless you have a clear idea of why you might need them. All kinds of things look useful, but ask yourself if you would actually use one if you had it.

▲ Grain-focusing magnifiers

A grain-focusing magnifier is another near-essential, allowing you to focus on the grain of the image, for maximum sharpness. On this Paterson, the eyepiece can be slid to and fro to suit your eyesight, and a sliding collar covers the mirror to protect it from dust.

Print washers

Prints can be washed in a tray, or even in the bath, provided they are not allowed to stick together, but a purpose-made print washer will allow faster, more reliable washing. Again, this is close to essential. This Paterson 'flat bed' is ideal for RC paper (see page 54) and can wash one 30 x 40-cm (12 x 16-in) sheet; or two 20 x 25-cm (8 x 10-in) ones; or four 12.2 x 18-cm (5 x 7-in) ones. Vertical-slot washers are often used for fibre-based paper.

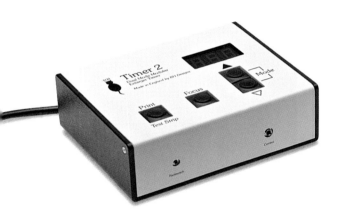

▼ Film wipers

To wipe films before drying, some use film squeegees (shown here), others chamois leathers; some run the film between forefinger and index finger; and others give the film a final rinse in wetting agent (see page 15), and let it dry without touching it.

◄ Enlarger timers

You can switch the enlarger on and off manually (or, preferably, with a foot switch), timing the exposure with a clock, but an enlarger timer is easier. This one is from RH Designs; there are many others, including the Paterson 2040. Most of the better models can be used with an accessory foot switch for 'hands-free' timing.

OTHER ACCESSORIES

An enlarger easel or masking frame makes it much easier to position paper for enlarging, and is all but essential. For more about these, see page 78.

Not essential, but extremely useful, is some form of paper dryer. For more about these, see page 60.

A light box makes it easier to examine and judge negatives before printing. Battery-powered units will do, but a small mains unit will give a more even light. Light boxes are also close to daylight colours, which makes them better for sorting slides.

Enlarging exposure meters can help you to judge the exposure that a print will need, and they can be surprisingly inexpensive: the Paterson EM1030 costs no more than half a dozen rolls of film. A full-blown enlarging analyzer will give both the exposure time and the contrast grade recommended, but costs a lot more and takes longer to learn to use.

▲ Mechanical timers

Mechanical timers are simple, and accurate enough for long exposures, but for short exposures (five seconds and under) they can be inconsistent. Ancient insulation can crack and crumble, so new timers are a better bet than elderly ones you may be given or may buy at camera fairs.

PROCESSING

It may sound obvious, but the foundation of a first-class print is a first-class negative — and it is quicker, cheaper and easier to produce first-class negatives yourself than it is to get them done professionally. Although it is possible to get a good print from a bad negative, it takes a good printer to do it, but if you start out with a good negative, it is often remarkably easy to make a good print.

Of course, a good negative starts long before you go into the darkroom. The classic problem for most beginners is under-exposure, leading to 'empty' shadows and thin negatives. To get around this, many increase development times in an attempt to 'push' the film, but this means that they still have empty shadows, plus coarser grain and overly-contrasty negatives. The best rule of thumb is attributed to photographic writer David Vestal: don't under-expose, and don't overdevelop.

CHOOSING FILM DEVELOPERS

Traditionally, developers were made up from powders and reused. With each subsequent batch of films, development times were increased (typically by about 10 per cent) to compensate for the exhaustion of the developer: as many as eight films might be developed in a single litre. Today, it is more usual (and more convenient, and safer, and more consistent) to use liquid 'one-shot' developers. These are diluted from a concentrate, used once, and then thrown away.

Different developers are designed for different applications, and without doubt, some films and some developers work better in combination than others. Quite apart from their objective qualities, different combinations of developer and film have different 'personalities', and it is often a question of pure chance whether you hit on a combination that suits you.

You have to strike a balance between endlessly searching for a (possibly illusory) Holy Grail, and persisting with a film/developer combination that clearly isn't working for you, even though it may have worked for someone else. For any given film, the best starting point for choosing a developer is to read the manufacturers' technical data sheets. These may be available from a photographic dealer, available from film and developer manufacturers on request, or found on the internet. In general, there are four choices:

Standard fine-grain developers give what most people regard as the optimum mixture of speed, grain and sharpness. The classic 'standard' developer is Kodak D-76/Ilford ID-11, but there are many more: Paterson's, for example, is Aculux. These developers are recommended for just about any film.

Ultra-fine-grain developers give finer grain, but invariably at the expense of film speed: you lose anything up to a stop, and sometimes even more. Like 'standard' developers, they can be used with most films and give the same sort of sharpness.

Acutance developers give maximum sharpness, with similar speed to 'standard', but normally with slightly coarser grain. They are most useful with slower, 'old-technology' films – ISO 200 and below – where the increase in sharpness will be most obvious and where a slight increase in grain does not matter.

Speed-increasing developers (also known as 'push' developers) give maximum film speeds – that is, maximum shadow detail – but with coarser grain and lower sharpness than 'standard'. They are recommended for faster films, ISO 400 and above.

◄ *Slow film, ultra-fine grain developer (Boonesboro Museum)*
For a picture like this, with lots of detail, you want a sharp, fine-grained film and a developer that will accentuate both these qualities. An ideal combination might be something like Ilford 100 Delta, rated at EI ('exposure index', see page 33) 80 or even 64, and developed in Paterson Acutol.

DILUTION

Many developers can be used at a choice of dilutions. Most Paterson developers are designed to be used at 1+9 (10 ml of developer to 90 ml of water) but they can also be used at 1+14, where longer developing times are desired, and at 1+19, at which they exhibit a compensating effect; in other words, they compress the highlights of subjects with a very long tonal range. Normally, maximum speed and finest grain are delivered at higher strengths, with more sharpness (but lower speed and coarser grain) at higher dilutions.

◄ *Fast film, 'push' developer (Folklore Museum, Gozo)*
Unexpectedly, Ilford Delta 3200 proved very useful for this picture. Light levels were very low, and there were a lot of people in the museum. The exposure time with a slow film would have been so long as to risk people walking into shot. To ensure reasonable shadow detail, the film was rated at EI 1600, about half a stop faster than its ISO speed, and developed in Paterson Varispeed, a 'push' developer.

Other types of developer are of limited application. Universal developers can be used for both film and paper, normally at different dilutions, but they give coarse grain, poor sharpness and often low speed. Two-bath, staining and high-energy developers have their uses, but many people attribute to them near-magical properties that they do not possess. Indeed, some old formulae may well deliver inferior results with modern materials, as compared to more conventional developers.

SPEEDS

Invariably, you will get finer grain by using a slower film and a speed-increasing developer rather than a faster film and a fine-grain developer — and film speeds may not be that much different either. For example, Ilford Pan F P us in a speed-increasing developer can give a true ISO 64 or even 80 (up from nominal 50), while Ilford FP4 Plus in a fine-grain developer may well drop to ISO 100 or even 80 (down from nominal 125) — and the Pan F will always be finer-grained.

DEVELOPMENT TIMES

Although we shall return to this point, we cannot over-emphasize that manufacturers' recommended development times are only a starting point. If you get better results at a different time — even if it is two-thirds as much — that is the development time to use.

▲ *Slow film, acutance developer (Wayside shrine, Malta)*
It is generally a good idea to use the slowest film you can for a particular application, as it will be sharper and finer-grained and less expensive. This is Ilford 100 Delta developed in Paterson FX39 for maximum sharpness: the film is so fine-grained that the slight increase in grain is not a problem with a 20 x 25-cm (8 x 10-in) print.

THE PERFECT NEGATIVE:
BASIC ASSUMPTIONS

Film speeds and exposure meters rely on a series of assumptions about 'average' subjects. The surprising thing is that they work as well and as often as they do, despite wide variations in total reflectivity and subject-brightness range; but if you understand the assumptions, it will help you get better negatives. It will also help you understand why it can be harder to get a 'perfect' black-and-white exposure than a 'perfect' colour exposure, 'perfect' being defined as 'exactly what you visualized'.

First, a meter is calibrated to an 'average' reflectivity. Different scenes reflect different amounts of light. A snowy landscape may reflect 90 per cent of the light falling on it; a black cat in a coal cellar just two per cent. Research indicates than an 'average' landscape reflects about 13 per cent of the light falling on it (not 18 per cent, as some believe). Meters are based on this assumption.

Next, the film-development recommendations have to be calibrated to an 'average' subject-brightness range. A brilliant landscape with the sun in shot and reflections on sparkling water may have a brightness range of 1,000,000:1, while the same landscape on a dull, overcast day may have a brightness range of 50:1 or less.

As a result of the research of the 1930s and 1940s mentioned above, an 'average' brightness range is normally taken as 128:1, or seven stops, and development recommendations for black–and–white films are based on this assumption.

A black-and-white negative can, on the other hand, capture an enormous brightness range – 1000:1 (10 stops) or more. Film speeds are therefore based on shadow detail: you don't have to use it, but it is there if you want it.

'Cart tracks', Malta

These prehistoric 'cart-track' ruts were cut over hundreds of years by stone-tipped runners, before the invention of the wheel. In this shot, where the distant buildings, wall and sky are a part of the image, a slightly harder-than-normal paper (grade 2½) was used to increase the differentiation of the ruts.

Close-up of 'cart tracks'

In this shot, taken, like the one on the left, on Ilford Delta 100, where only the low-contrast ruts themselves are of interest, a still harder grade (3½) allowed even better differentiation. Contrast is an aesthetic choice, not scientific, and often it is also a compromise.

There are three ways to bridge the gap between a negative with a 1000:1 brightness range, and a print with 100:1. First, you can print so that the brightness range of the final image is close to the brightness range of an 'average' subject, at something between 64:1 and 128:1 (i.e. 6–7 stops), and live without brighter highlights and darker shadows. Second, you can use a softer grade of paper so that the longer tonal range of the negative is compressed when printed. Third, you can dodge and burn locally (see page 72).

Using the latter two, you can often represent a subject-brightness range of as much as 250:1 (roughly 8 stops) convincingly in a black-and-white print. It is possible to represent still wider brightness ranges, but often the print will look flat and unnatural, and you will do better either to lose some of the tonal range of the negative, or to dodge and burn.

COLOUR

Colour is another matter. Colours can only be represented across a short brightness range – as little as 32:1. Colour images therefore have to lose part of the brightness range of the subject. The choice is between good shadow detail, with the highlights 'blown' or washed-out, and good highlight detail, with dark shadows. The latter usually looks much better, so film speeds for slides are based on the highlights. Most in-camera meters are designed to give good exposures with slide film. For more about how to get around this, see pages 32–33.

Although colour prints can only represent a limited tonal range, the intermediate step of a negative means that you can still expose for the shadow detail, then choose what to represent on the print, as with black and white.

▶ *Waterfall, Kodaikanal, India*
The tonal range of this scene, a waterfall under brilliant tropical light in the south of India, is well over 1000:1. There are two ways to treat it. One is to try to compress the tonal range: you can do this either by printing on a soft paper grade, or by over-exposing the negative (about two stops extra) and then under-developing it (about two-thirds of the normal time), which will give you a less-contrasty negative. The other approach – which looks more natural in our opinion – is to print so that the extreme contrast is retained in the final picture, with the sparkling water contrasting against the dark area.

THE PERFECT NEGATIVE: METERING AND EXPOSURE

If you give a negative plenty of exposure, you will have all the shadow detail you could wish for, and you will often get the tonality and 'richness' that most people prefer. On the other hand, generous exposure also means coarser grain and reduced sharpness, and minimum exposure also means that you can have more depth of field (from a smaller aperture) or better action-stopping and less risk of camera shake (from a faster shutter speed), or both.

'Correct' exposure is a compromise between finest grain and maximum sharpness, but no shadow detail, and good shadow detail, but impaired grain and sharpness.

With 35mm, which we have assumed that most readers of this book will use, this compromise is important. With larger formats, you can afford to sacrifice both grain and sharpness, because the negatives are normally enlarged less: many photographers cheerfully give half a stop or a stop (or sometimes more) of extra exposure with larger formats, as compared with 35mm.

METERING FOR MONOCHROME

Only you can decide how much shadow detail you want, but as we have already seen, meters are normally designed for giving good exposure with slides and may result in loss of shadow detail unless you change your metering technique. There are three ways of doing this: true spot metering, limited area metering, and simply resetting the film speed.

SPOT METERING

The ultimate tool for exposure in black and white is a spot meter. You take a reading of the darkest area in which you want shadow detail, then set this reading against the shadow index on the meter scale – here, the IRE 1 (shadow) index. You would use the IRE 5 index if you wanted to key your exposure to a mid-tone, and IRE 10 if you wanted to key it to the highlight.

No shadow detail

There is no detail at all in the shadows in this negative. You might be able to make a contrasty, graphic print from it, but you will never get a richly textured image. What isn't there on the negative can't be there on the print.

Good shadow detail

There is plenty of detail in the shadows of this 4 x 5-in negative, because it has received around a stop more than the optimum exposure for 35mm, and maybe two stops more than most in-camera meters would recommend.

Many newcomers to spot metering waste a lot of time trying to guess what part of the subject might be a 'mid-tone' and reading that, when metering the shadows is quick, easy and reliable. The only drawback is that spot meters are very expensive. If you use a spot meter and base your exposure on the shadows, you can normally rely on the full ISO film speed.

LIMITED-AREA METERING

Spot-meter options in camera meters will normally cover a wider angle than a true spot meter, but with any meter, you can simply go in close and meter the shadow areas, taking care not to shade the area you are metering. This is limited-area metering. As with true spot metering, read the darkest area in which you want shadow detail. If you followed this reading blindly, though, the result would be over-exposure. Because you are metering shadows, you want them to be darker than the 'average' exposure, so give less exposure than the meter indicates – try two stops. If there still isn't enough shadow detail, try 1½ stops less with your next film; if there is plenty of shadow detail, try 2½ stops next time.

RESETTING THE FILM SPEED

Most people find that they can get better exposures on negative film, even with auto-exposure cameras, by setting their in-camera or hand-held meter to an exposure index (EI) that is one half of the film speed: for example, EI 50 for an ISO 100 film, EI 200 for an ISO 400 film. The term 'EI' is used because ISO speeds are scientifically defined, while EI speeds are simply a question of what works for you, and are not fixed: where one person uses EI 50 for an ISO 100 film, others might use EI 40, or 64 or 80.

▲ *Civil War interior*
A good shadow area to read here would be to the right of the trunk at the foot of the bed; another possibility would be the fireplace. The film was Ilford XP2.

▲ *Squirrel*
This squirrel in Washington Square, New York City, would almost certainly have been underexposed had the meter been set to the full film speed for Ilford XP2, ISO 400, instead of ISO 250.

Pentax spot meter
IRE 1 is the shadow index. You would use IRE 5 index if you wanted a mid-tone reading, and IRE 10 for a highlight reading.

THE PERFECT NEGATIVE:

DEVELOPMENT AND PAPER GRADE

As we have already seen, manufacturers' development recommendations should deliver good negatives of 'average' subjects. A 'good' negative is one that prints well on a middling grade of paper, typically 2 or 3 (see page 50).

Suppose, though, that your subject is not 'average'. For example, if you are shooting landscapes on a dull day, 'average' development may well result in flat, dull negatives that require a hard grade of paper (see page 50) to print well. For pictures taken on a bright, sunny day at the beach, on the other hand, 'average' development may give contrasty negatives that require a soft grade of paper to print well.

If you shoot a whole roll under one set of conditions, or if negatives show consistent departures from 'average', you might do well to give 50 per cent more than 'average' development for subjects with a short brightness range (such as a dull day), and 15 per cent less for subjects with a long brightness range (such as a sunny beach). This '15/50' rule is only a rough guideline, but it should give better negatives.

Of course, most people do not shoot a whole roll under one set of lighting conditions: the subjects are mixed, so you have to give 'average'

development and change paper grades to suit non-'average' subjects. And, of course, you should dodge and burn locally (see page 72) to hold detail that might otherwise disappear.

If you have got your development about right, you should find that most of your 'average' subjects require something around grade 2 or 3, with harder grades (4 and maybe 5) for the low-contrast subjects and softer grades (1 and maybe 0) for the high-contrast subjects.

If you find yourself consistently using (say) grades 0, 1 and 2, but almost never 3 and 4, your negatives are too contrasty and you would probably benefit from giving a little less development in future. If you constantly need grades 4 and even 5, your negatives are too soft, and you would probably get better results from giving a little more development in future. A need for grades 4 and 5 may also indicate underexposure, so look hard at the shadow detail (the light areas) on the negative itself. If there is no texture or detail in the shadows, you are underexposing and you should reset your film speed to a lower value (see page 33). As a general rule, you should increase or decrease development times in

◀ *Old Rope Works, Chatham Dockyard*

The exposure here (on Ilford Delta 3200) was based on a limited area reading from the drive motor in the box on the left. The window on the right was at least 500 times brighter, and was 'blown' on a straight print; but a little burning in (see page 72) meant that the glazing bars between the panes of glass were recaptured and rendered convincingly.

▲ Snerab Ling

Frances photographed Sherab Ling, the 'Place of Wisdom', on Ilford XP2 Super. This normally prints best on paper half a grade more contrasty than is needed with a non-chromogenic film. On this occasion, she went a further half-grade harder (i.e. a full grade harder) to recapture some of the subject that was lost in dust and haze. Printing is a subjective process, not objective.

▶ Mertola, Portugal

With infrared or extended-red film – this example is on Ilford SFX – all bets are off, as tonal values are wildly distorted from their 'real' values, and in this case the only guide to printing is what looks good.

increments of 30 second (for development times up to seven minutes), or one minute (for development times of eight minutes and beyond). Always round to the nearest 30 seconds: if 15 seconds makes much difference, your development time is too short.

TEMPERATURE

The warmer the developer, the further you can cut development times. Most development times are specified at 20° or 24°C (68° or 75°F): at 20°C (68°F), you typically need two-thirds of the development time at 24°C (75°F). Manufacturers normally supply a chart or nomogram for other temperatures: the representative sample reproduced here [right] will work for most developers. Across the range of 18– 24°C (65–75°F), there should not be much variation in tonality, provided you make the appropriate time compensation, but outside this range you may find that negatives start to go more or less contrasty, and effective film speed may change.

Mix the developer as close to the right temperature as possible by using warm or chilled water, and adjust the final temperature with a bath of warm water or ice water – not by adding ice cubes or boiling water to the developer!

AGITATION

More agitation is the same as more time or a higher temperature. If you agitate continuously, you should decrease your development time by 10–15 per cent as compared with normal agitation (defined as five seconds every 30 seconds, or 10 seconds every 60 seconds).

TIME AND TEMPERATURE

Development times are normally defined for a temperature of 20°C (68°F). For other temperatures, change the times as indicated.

	18°C (64°F)	20°C (68°F)	22°C (71°F)	24°C (75°F)
MINUTES	3.25	**3**	2.5	2
	5	**4**	3.25	2.5
	6.25	**5**	4	3
	7.5	**6**	4.5	3.5
	8.75	**7**	5	4.25
	10	**8**	6.5	5
	11.25	**9**	7.25	5.5
	12.5	**10**	8	6
	13.75	**11**	9	6.5
	15	**12**	9.5	7.25
	16.25	**13**	10.5	8
	17.5	**14**	11.25	8.5
	18.75	**15**	12	9
	20	**16**	12.75	9.5

SHORT STOP AND FIXER

After development, already described on pages 14–15, a short stop (which is optional) arrests the action of the developer and prolongs the fixer life, and the fixer dissolves out the unexposed silver halide.

SHORT STOP

The short stop should be diluted as directed – for example, 1 part to 39 for Paterson's Acustop – and used at the same temperature as the developer and fixer. If the short stop is too strong, it may have adverse effects on image quality, including even pin-holes on the image, though it would need to be several times too strong to cause this effect with modern films. If the temperature varies too much, there is a danger of 'reticulation' or puckering of the gelatine as a result of thermal shock, but again, this is not much of a risk with modern films – in fact, when we tried to get a modern Ilford film to reticulate, to show what the effect looked like for this book, we couldn't.

Although short stop can be reused repeatedly, the exact capacity (the amount of film it can process) varies widely, according to various factors: the alkalinity of the developer, the amount of developer carried over into the short stop, and the strength of short stop, as well as its composition.

◀ *When to stop*

'Indicator' short-stop baths are easiest to use, as they are simply reused until they change colour.

Yellow = OK   Purple = exhausted

💡 fixing times and fixer exhaustion

Dilute the fixer to the chosen strength and adjust the temperature with a water bath if needed. Before you load the film into the spiral for processing, cut off the leader 'tongue' (see page 38), and use this for the test.

This gives you the 'clearing time' for this particular film. Fix the film for at least twice the clearing time, and at most three times; this is the 'fixing time'. Repeat this test each time you reuse the fixer. When the clearing time (and

hence the fixing time) is twice that for fresh fixer with the same film, throw it away and mix up a new batch. Very roughly, 1 l (36 fl oz) of working-strength fixer should fix 25–30 35mm films. The main variables are the level of exposure – over-exposed films have less silver to fix out than under-exposed ones – and the sort of film you use: fast films generally have more silver than slow ones, and 'old-technology' films more silver than 'new-technology'.

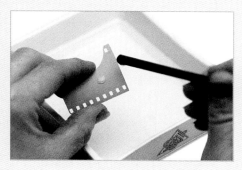

1 Place one drop of fixer on the leader and let it act for 10–20 seconds.

2 Immerse the whole strip of film in the fixer...

3 ... and time how long it takes until you can no longer see the spot.

urless short stops are based on citric acid instead of acetic acid
(basic ingredient of vinegar) and are more pleasant to use but
not be re-used as often. The film does not need to be in the short
for long: 30 seconds (or even 15) is adequate, and 60 seconds is
e than enough.

ERS

the same reasons as short stop, the fixer should be close to the
perature of the developer. Unlike developers, fixers last for months,
at working strength, and can be reused repeatedly.

Most photographers today use 'rapid' fixers, which can fix a film
ral times as fast as plain 'hypo' (sodium thiosulphate). Often, two
ions are given, one for ultra-rapid action and one for slower action:
weaker solution is cheaper to use, even though it will not process
e so many films. Either dilution can be tested as described below
as can the required fixing time. Cheap (but equally efficient) fixers
be made up from powders, but these are inconvenient and the

health risk from the dust means that liquid concentrates are generally a
better idea.

Precise fixing times vary enormously. Slow film in fresh, strong fixer
will fix fastest, sometimes in 30 seconds or less, while fast films in well-
used, weak fixer may well take three minutes or even more. Likewise,
the rate of exhaustion can vary quite a lot: fast films typically exhaust
the fixer more rapidly, as do under-exposed films, where there is more
undeveloped silver to be fixed out.

▼ *Working with light tones*

*In this picture, shot in Malta on Ilford SFX and developed in
Paterson Varispeed, there is considerable differentiation of the
very light tones in the building. Over-fixing would bleach out these
very pale greys and spoil the picture. Leaving prints in the fixer for
20 minutes or more, until you are ready to wash them, is a very
bad idea: a tray full of plain water is a much safer 'holding tank'.*

PROCESSING FILMS

Processing your own film is not only cheaper than going to a commercial laboratory, it is also a lot quicker. It takes less than half an hour to load and process a film, from walking into the darkroom to pinning the film up to dry (see pages 40–41). In fact, it takes only a few minutes longer to process two films, as many film tanks can hold more than one film spiral.

Before you start, make sure you have everything you need. This includes the film itself; the tank — make sure you have all the parts (see page 16), and that the spiral is bone dry otherwise the film will stick as it is loaded into the spiral; a film cassette opener (an old-fashioned bottle-opener works fine), and a pair of scissors. You also need a dust-free work surface big enough to lay everything out ready for use.

 ## loading the tank

The film must be loaded into the tank in absolute darkness, or it will be fogged by stray light. It is a good idea to practise beforehand in daylight, with a scrap film. Although you should normally handle the film only by the edges, you may find it easiest to pinch the very end between thumb and forefinger and pull it into the spiral, rather than trying to push it in.

The main risks are fingerprints — damp, dirty, greasy or sweaty fingers leave clear, irremovable marks; some people wear cotton or surgical gloves, though this makes handling much more difficult — and stress marks, crescent-shaped marks which result from pinching the film too tightly. If you start off badly, don't try to correct matters: pull the film out carefully and start again.

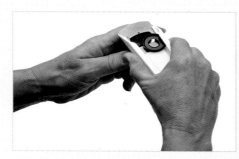

1 Open the film cassette. Generally, it is easiest to open the 'short' end where the centre spool does not poke through. The end cap just pops off.

2 Pull the spool out of the cassette, and cut the tongue off the film. Save it for a fixer test (page 36).

3 Push or pull the end of the film into the 'jaws' of the spiral. You will feel a slight resistance, then it should feed in smoothly.

4 Rotate one side of the spiral relative to the other until it stops. Rotate it back until it stops.

5 Cut the end of the film off the spool and finish winding it on.

6 Put the spiral into the tank. Check (by touch) that all light traps are in place. Put on the lid

processing

This can be done in normal room lighting. Again, make sure you have everything you need, including the loaded tank; the chemicals – the developer (see pages 28–29), stop bath (if used, see pages 36–37) and fixer (see pages 36–37); a thermometer and timer (see page 18–19); and a working surface where a few splashes will not matter. Check the developer instruction leaflet for the development time: depending on the film and developer used, and the temperature, this can range from five to 15 minutes. Remember, too, that higher temperatures mean shorter developing times, while lower temperatures mean longer developing times, as detailed on page 35.

USEFUL TIPS

• Some people agitate the tank for five seconds per minute instead of five seconds every 30 seconds – it doesn't matter which you do, as long as you are consistent.

• If you use a non-hardening fixer (see glossary) and if the film has been processed at 24°C (75°F) or below, save time and water as follows. Fill the tank with clean water at the same temperature as the other chemicals, invert five times, and drain. Fill again; invert ten times and drain. Fill again; invert 20 times and drain. The film is now fully washed.

1 Mix the chemistry as described on pages 29 and 36. Check the temperature (normally 20°C/68°F or 24°C/75°F).

2 Remove the outer lid of the tank, and tip in the developer, quickly and smoothly. Start the clock. Rap the tank sharply on the table to dislodge any air bubbles, which otherwise will leave undeveloped circles on the film.

3 If your tank has a spiral agitation spindle, insert and rotate alternately clockwise and anticlockwise for 15 seconds. Then replace the lid and agitate by inversion as described next.

Inset: If your tank has no agitation spindle, replace the lid immediately and invert the tank smoothly, about once per second, for the first 15 seconds, then for five seconds every 30 seconds.

4 About 15-20 seconds before the end of the developing time, pour out the developer. Drain for 5–10 seconds. Pour in the short stop (if used) and agitate for 15 seconds. Drain after 30 seconds and pour in the fixer. If you are not using short stop, pour in the fixer and agitate for 15 seconds, then five seconds every 30 seconds. Drain after the recommended time (see page 37).

5 Wash with running water for at least five minutes: inadequately washed films will fade and stain, often patchily. The best ways to dry the film, and to avoid smears, marks and scratches, are given overleaf.

DRYING, SLEEVING AND STORAGE

Drying film is normally dismissed in a few words in most books on photography, which is why so many people end up with dirty, scratched or smeary negatives. A few minutes' attention at this stage can save hours of spotting out dust marks (see page 88) later on, to say nothing of the anguish of discovering, when you try to print what looks like a beautiful negative, that there is a huge scratch running down it.

Sleeving and storage are a chore, but if you start out by doing things properly, you will find it much easier than trying to impose order on a chaotic mass of negatives later on, when you have scores or hundreds of films instead of just a handful.

DRYING

Drying begins with a final rinse in water containing wetting agent, which is rather like a very dilute detergent. This helps the water to flow smoothly off the negative, without leaving drops that dry to chalky marks. In hard-water areas, it is a good idea to use distilled or purified water.

Take the film out of the tank and fill the tank with clean, fresh water. Add wetting agent according to the manufacturer's instructions: normally, around one part to 500 of water. Mix well. Put the film back

in the tank, and agitate for 30–60 seconds. Do not agitate too hard, or you will get froth.

Take the film off the spiral, handling it only by the edges. The emulsion is very tender at this stage, and easily scratched. If you wipe it with a squeegee or wet chamois leather, it must be scrupulously clean. Many photographers prefer not to touch the emulsion at all at this stage.

If possible, pin the film up diagonally in a dust-free area: across a doorway is ideal. Water will run down to the edge of the film, which will dry cleaner and faster as a result. Do not stretch it too tightly, as it will shrink slightly as it dries – enough to tear through one film perforation.

(see page 88)

useful tip

- After removing the film and pinning it up to dry, wash the tank spiral immediately. Some wetting solutions seem to attack and roughen certain plastics, while others leave a residue. Either makes loading more difficult.

◄ *Pinning film diagonally*

As you pin the film up, leave a couple of sprocket holes at one end, to reduce the risk of catastrophe in the event of shrinkage and tearing (or just clumsy handling). At one end, as an added refinement, use a paper clip and an elastic band to keep the film under tension. If there is nowhere you can pin the film diagonally, hang it up vertically. The bathroom is often a good place to dry film, as the steam lays the dust.

▼ *Film dryers*

You can buy various types of film dryer, like this Nova. The 'skirt' below the fan box extends to protect the film; filtered, warmed air is blown down from the top. Use a heavy film clip, or the film may wobble and stick to the side of the dryer.

SLEEVING AND STORAGE

Many types of sleeves are available, but the best are probably polyethylene multi-pocket sleeves that are loaded from one end. Be sure to get the sort that can accommodate seven strips of six exposures each: some will only accept seven strips of five. A great advantage of polyethylene sleeves is that you can make contact prints (see page 64) through the sleeve. With an indelible laundry marker or something similar, write on the sleeve at least the date; the developer and development

regime (e.g. FX-39, 1+9, 7 min, 20°); and where the pictures were taken. If you are more organized you can add accession numbers or anything else you think useful. The sleeves themselves can be stored in ring binders, preferably filed with the contact prints.

Even if you dried the film diagonally, hang it up vertically for cutting and sleeving. This is less risky than resting it on a (possibly dusty) table. Pin the black leader end of the film at the top, and cut off the waste at the bottom end of the film.

archival sleeves

Polyethylene sleeves, such as the Print File holders shown here, are often described as 'archival' because they are inert and contain nothing that can harm the film. Cheaper plastic, and paper or 'glassine' sleeves may lead eventually to patchy fading and spotting of the image.

Always make sure that the negatives are absolutely bone dry before you put them away. If they are wet, they normally stick and refuse to go in, and it is then very difficult to dry the interior of the sleeve, especially without spreading dust or lint. Worse still, they sometimes go in, stick, and then cannot be removed later without damage.

1 Trim off the corners of the end of the film as shown. This is not essential, but it can make them much easier to push into the sleeves.

2 Cut off the film in strips of six frames. A few holders take seven strips of five frames, but this is purgatory if you normally use 36-exposure films instead of 20 or 24.

3 Working from the bottom of the sleeve, push the first strip in. The advantage of starting at the last frame is that if you have 37 or 38 exposures, you can use some of the leader to ensure that you have a reasonably long final strip.

4 Box-type files help to keep dust away from the negatives. Some people file purely in date order, while others separate their negatives into categories.

TRADE-PROCESSED FILM — AND C-41

Very few labs can reliably process black-and-white films. There are so many films, and so many developers, that most labs operate a 'one size fits all' policy. If you want to have your film trade-processed, there are four possibilities.

The first is to find a good professional lab. Ask them what sort of film they process best, and at what speed they recommend that you rate it. This will almost invariably be lower than the nominal ISO speed, because of the developers. Follow their advice, and be prepared to pay well.

The second is to scan the photo magazines for a small lab or private individual who caters to monochrome users, and follow much the same route, except that it shouldn't cost you quite so much.

The third, in countries where the service is available, is to use the Ilford pre-paid mailer service, preferably with Ilford film, and ideally with Ilford HP5 Plus.

The fourth is to use a C-41-compatible film. These are also known as 'chromogenic' films because they use the same technology as colour-print

◀ *Chromogenic films*

The difference in tonality between Ilford's chromogenic and conventional films has been described by Ilford themselves as the difference between 'smooth' and 'gnarly'. This 19th-century library was shot on XP1 in the 1980s, and the negative was well over a decade old when it was printed for this book: there is no truth in the belief that chromogenic films will not last as long as conventional films.

films. You can even use a mini-lab and get your negatives, plus reference prints, back in one hour, though the prints may have strange colour casts from being printed on colour paper.

The longest-established chromogenic film on the market is Ilford XP2 Super; this is a descendant of the original XP1 from the early 1980s. In addition, there are two alternatives available from Kodak (T400CN and Select B & W), and Konica offers VX400. Kodak's film is the finest-grained option, but Ilford's is sharper and most people prefer its tonality, especially in the highlights.

All of these films are nominally ISO 400, though the Ilford film is nearer ISO 500, and all are far finer-grained than their speed suggests, comparable with conventional ISO 100 films.

Although in theory any lab that can process C-41 can process chromogenic black-and-white films, the difficulty lies in finding a lab that can deliver clean negatives, free of dust and fingerprints.

The only way to be sure is to take work to a number of different labs. Price is no guide to quality: the results from some supermarket or high-street chemists' labs are excellent, and those from some professional labs are terrible.

As already mentioned, 'proofs' made on colour paper may be oddly coloured – we have seen sepia, green, violet and some other colours – but they are at least a useful guide to what you have got, and at best, they are usable prints. Kodak's films tend to print with more neutral colours than Ilford's.

You may have to point to the place on the cassette where it says 'process C-41', because inexperienced mini-lab operators may say, 'No, we aren't set up to handle black and white film, we can only do colour.' Some can take quite a bit of convincing that C-41 monochrome films are compatible with C-41 colour chemistry.

If all else fails, show them this book.

◄ *Using contrast*
Kodak's T400CN tends to suffer from runaway contrast in the highlights, but with the right subject this can be exploited to good effect. With Ilford XP2 Super there would be much more tone behind the catkins, and the picture would be less dramatic. This would make a great lith print (see page 112).

HOW DO CHROMOGENIC FILMS HANDLE?

Chromogenic films are exposed in the same way as ordinary films, and respond to filters in much the same way. As with silver films, increased exposure means reduced sharpness, but unlike conventional films, increased exposure means decreased grain. Also, if you print them using old-fashioned condenser enlargers, they deliver the same contrast as they do with diffuser enlargers – unlike conventional films, which are more contrasty when printed with a condenser enlarger.

TROUBLESHOOTING NEGATIVES

The test for the perfect negative is easy: it makes a perfect print. Imperfect negatives range from the hard-to-print, via the unprintable, to the non-existent. When you start out in photography, it can be difficult to determine where you went wrong and why your negatives are not perfect.

It is probably best to look at the worst cases first, but it is important to emphasize two things. The first is that you need to be a long way out in both exposure and development before a negative is unprintable. The second is that most other problems are the result of easily avoidable mistakes. The examples on these pages show common mistakes and suggest remedies for avoiding these problems in the future.

Incidentally, it is worth mentioning that although a few of the negatives on these pages were specially made for this book, most were simply pulled from our early files. Everyone makes every mistake in the book, sooner or later...

DICHROIC STAINS

One fault, not illustrated here because it is very hard to show but very easy to describe, is a dichroic stain. This is a stain that is one colour by reflected light and another by transmitted light – typically cyan/green one way, and red/magenta the other. It is very rare nowadays, but is normally caused by unsuitable developer, or too-long development in overdiluted developer.

How close is close enough?

You can still get surprisingly good results from films that have received two stops more exposure than they should, or two stops less, or that have been developed for twice as long as necessary, or half as long. Indeed, many people prefer the results they get from over-exposed, under-developed negatives, or from under-exposed, overdeveloped ones, though there is less appeal in negatives that have been both under-exposed and underdeveloped or over-exposed and overdeveloped.

▲ **Completely blank film with no edge markings**
The film has not been developed. Either the developer was completely exhausted, or the fixer was poured in before the developer.
Remedy: *Take more care next time!*

▲ **Blank film with edge markings**
The film has not been exposed. Either it was not loaded properly, or the camera is defective.
Remedy: *Check camera; make sure rewind knob rotates on mechanical cameras.*

▲ **Film partially or uniformly black**
'Light strike', typically as a result of the camera back being opened without rewinding. Thin strips of black suggest loading/unloading in very bright light, which struck through the velvet lips of the cassette.
Remedy: *Take more care!*

▲ **Film grey and muddy**
Film loaded into the developing tank in unsafe lighting.
Remedy: *Check black-out or use a changing bag next time (see page 17).*

◄ **Thin negatives without shadow detail**
Under-exposure in camera (see page 32). Will print on normal paper, but without shadow detail.
Remedy: *Increase exposure next time (decrease film-speed setting on meter).*

◄ **Thin negatives with shadow detail**
Under-development. Should print satisfactorily on hard paper.
Remedy: *Increase development time next time.*

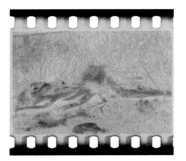

▲ **Brown stains begin to appear on dry negatives**

Inadequate fixing or washing, or both.
Remedy: Always fix for the proper length of time (see page 37) and wash adequately (see page 39).

▲ **Milky haze on all or part of negative**

Inadequate fixing. May be possible to cure by refixing in fresh fixer and rewashing.
Remedy: Fix for the right length of time (see page 37).

▲ **Contrasty negatives**

Overdevelopment. Should print satisfactorily on soft paper.
Remedy: Reduce development next time.

▲ **Very dense negatives**

Over-exposure.
Remedy: Reduce exposure next time.

▲ **Stress marks**

Crescent-shaped marks caused by stress during loading.
Remedy: Avoid crimping or kinking film.

▲ **Creamy blotches on film**

The developing tank was loaded improperly so that two adjacent areas of film were in contact, and the developer and fixer were unable to reach the emulsion. This happens only with stainless-steel reels.
Remedy: Practise loading with a scrap film.

▲**Drying marks**

Dissolved solids in the water leave marks as the water evaporates.
Remedy: Use distilled water for the final rinse; hang film diagonally if possible, so that drips run into rebate.

▲ **Thin, contrasty negatives**

Under-exposure plus overdevelopment.
Remedy: Give more exposure next time, and cut development time.

▲ **Reticulation**

Reticulation consists of small 'pucker' marks on film, and is caused by too wide a difference in the temperatures of processing solutions (or, very rarely, by the use of unsuitable developers or fixers). This 4 x 5-in film was inadvertently washed under the hot tap!
Remedy: Keep all solutions within 2–3° of one another.

INTENSIFIERS AND REDUCERS

Years ago, photographers rescued under-exposed and under-developed negatives via 'intensifiers', and reduced the density of over-exposed negatives with 'reducers'. These after-baths for exposed, developed negatives were acceptable in the days of big glass plates, but with roll-film negatives the use is limited, and with 35mm they give appalling image quality. Also, while some reducers are not too dangerous, the more effective intensifiers use toxic chemicals such as mercuric chloride and uranium nitrate.

THE DARKROOM NOTEBOOK

It is much easier to keep track of problems, as well as of successes, if you keep a darkroom notebook. There is absolutely no need to make a note of every picture you make (though some people do), but it is very useful to know what film and developer you used, at what concentration and temperature, and with what agitation. For example, a typical entry in our notebooks might read: '12/12/99–3 & 4 – Ilford 100 Delta (35), Paterson FX-39 1+9, 7 min, 20.1 in, 20.4 out, 22 ambient, 5/30; 2 reel SS.'

This gives the date; the films developed that day (here, the third and fourth, hence '–3 & 4' on the end of the date); the film type and format (many photographers have different development times for 35mm, roll film and sheet film); the developer and dilution; the time of development; the temperature when the developer was poured in (in this case 20.1°C); the temperature when it was poured out; the room, or ambient temperature (this may seem like perfectionism, but it only takes a couple

of seconds to note and to write down, and helps us to keep an eye on temperature drift); the agitation – five seconds every 30 seconds; and the tank type, in this case a two-reel stainless-steel tank.

Under this entry we will leave a line or two blank, so that later we can add 'Printed OK on MG IV' (Ilford Multigrade IV) or 'Too contrasty – needed grade 1' or whatever, if we remember. The date and film number then become the accession or filing number of that particular roll of film, written on the sleeve (see page 41).

▼ Easing the burden

Without a lab notebook, there are all too many things to remember, too many things to confuse with one another. Writing things down increases the chances of remembering how you did it last time, and reduces the number of things you have to keep separate in your mind.

useful tips

REFERRING TO THE NOTEBOOK

• Use different coloured highlighter pens for different topics – blue for film, pink for developer, and so on.

• Consider running two separate notebooks, one for film development and one for detailed printing.

FILM DEVELOPMENT:
14/2/98–1 and 2 – Paterson Acupan 200
(35) @ 125, FX39, 5 ½ min, 20.1 in/20.6
out, 23 ambient, 5/30; 2-reel SS

PRINT
14/2/98–2–16a, Mertola Castle, 8 x 10 all
in, 20 cm, 20 sec f/8, MG WT, 1 stop burn'

▶ *Notes for improving*

When you get a print that you particularly like, make sure that you have notes in the darkroom notebook of everything you can remember. We initially made notes on the film development and printing of this picture (see top right) and later added 'toned selenium' to the print entry, and 'Nikon F, 35–85' to the film-development entry to remind ourselves of camera and lens.

PRINTING DETAILS

The same notebook, or another volume, can be used for recording printing details. The negative will normally be given its accession number, frame number and a brief description, such as '12/12/99–1 – 24a/25, Sophie smiling', so that 24a/25 is the frame number beside the negative and we know what the subject was.

The entry might then read, '12/12/99–1 – 24a/25, Sophie smiling, 8 x 10 all in, 20 cm, 15 sec f/5.6+½ MG WT', where '8 x 10 all in' means that the image was printed 'all in' (without cropping) on 8 x 10 in at a column elevation of 20 cm, and that the required exposure was 15 sec at the half stop between f/5.6 and f/8 (hence 'f/5.6+½') on Ilford Multigrade Warmtone. Reprinting on another paper would mean longer or shorter exposure times, but at least this gives a good starting point. There may also be notes on cropping, dodging and burning (see page 72) and even toning (see page 94).

OTHER INFORMATION

Other information that can be put in the notebook includes dates that developers were made up or new bottles opened (though it is easier to write the latter on the cap with a soft pencil); dates that new bulbs were installed in enlargers or safelights, or new equipment bought or used for the first time; formulae from magazines or borrowed books; suggestions about developers or development times from fellow photographers (sample entry, 'DAVE reckons you should develop Delta 100 DD-X 1+9 for 11 min/20° – EI 80'); and even competition entry notes. Looking back over 20- and 30-year-old notes can be very enlightening!

BASIC PRINTING

Experienced printers make a distinction between 'work' prints and 'final' prints. You start off by making a straight 'work' print, then look at it to see what you could do to make it better. For many purposes, of course, the first or work print will be good enough for the final or exhibition print: certainly, it is likely to be better than the vast majority of commercial prints.

There is, however, the indisputable point that black-and-white photography is as much a matter of alchemy as of science – and as much a matter of luck as of alchemy. There is an enormous choice of papers and paper developers; negatives made by different photographers; different types of enlarger and enlarger lenses; and personal preference and individual technique. The only hope is to understand what you are doing, and why: flailing around aimlessly, never using the same materials twice, is a sure recipe for disaster.

PAPER CHOICE

Paper choice is part aesthetic and part technical, and different people have different priorities. Tonality is the most difficult and subjective question of all, for the reasons given below. The choice between fibre-based (FB) and resin-coated (RC) paper is considered on page 54, along with image colour and paper surfaces. Arguably, though, paper grade, considered on this page, is the most important factor in making an informed choice.

We have already seen that negatives can be 'normal' or 'contrasty' or 'flat'. In practice, of course, this refers to the results they would give when printed on 'normal' paper: a contrasty negative on soft (low-contrast) paper can still give a very good print, while a 'flat' (low-contrast) negative can be redeemed with the help of 'hard' (contrasty) paper.

The very softest grade, normally obtainable only with some variable-contrast papers, is grade 00: it is not illustrated here. Most papers start at grade 0 (very soft) or 1 (soft) and go up to grade 5. From time to time there are even harder papers than a conventional grade 5 – Agfa used to make a paper with an ISO(R) of around 30 – but their intermittent availability reflects their limited usefulness.

Not all papers are made in all grades: some are available in one grade only, normally grade 2. Because different manufacturers' contrast grades do not always match precisely, it is useful, if you can, to find the ISO(R) contrast of an unfamiliar paper from the manufacturers' specification sheets. How this is determined is not important here, but it provides a rigorous basis for comparing contrast. The higher the ISO(R), the lower the contrast of the paper.

MAXIMUM BLACK AND THE 'SILVER-RICH' MYTH

A good paper should be able to deliver a good, rich maximum black. It might seem logical that the more silver in a paper – the higher the 'coating weight' – the better the maximum black should be. Intuitive as this may seem, it is quite untrue. At least as important as coating weight is what the manufacturers call 'covering power'. Put crudely, small crystals pack together better, 'lose' the light more effectively, and give a better maximum black.

Most modern papers run around 1.6–1.8 grams per square metre (gsm) of silver; in one test, a paper with a coating weight of under 1.5 gsm achieved a significantly better maximum black than another with a coating weight of over 2.0 gsm.

Density ranges are expressed as a logarithm, so if the brightest part of a print (paper-base white) reflects 100 times more light than the darkest, they are 2.0 log density units apart: 2.0 is the logarithm of 100.

With the best glossy modern papers, density ranges of 2.2 and above (160:1) are attainable, though matt papers rarely exceed 1.6 (40:1). Older books often give 1.6 as a typical range for glossy papers.

ISO(R)

ISO(R) is the three-figure log exposure range of the paper – the exposure which will give a full tonal range from black to white – to two significant figures, with the decimal point removed. Thus an ISO(R) of 110 will give a full tonal range when exposed to a projected image with a brightness range of 1.10 ($3\frac{2}{3}$ stops).

PAPER SPEEDS

Although there is an ISO standard for paper speeds, just as there is for film speeds, hardly anyone uses it – after all, you get the best exposure on paper by trial and error. The fastest enlarging papers are about twice as fast as the slowest, though, so you may need to change exposures when you change papers.

Paper speeds may vary from grade to grade (hard papers are normally slower) and, depending on the manufacturer, from box to box.

TONALITY

Tonality is almost entirely subjective, but it is also a question of habit. Whenever manufacturers bring out a new paper that is unquestionably better in every way than the one it replaces, they seem to get nothing but endless moans from people who had got used to the shortcomings of the older material and had either adapted their working methods to suit its deficiencies or had simply persuaded themselves that they liked things that way.

There are other considerations that can lead to problems with paper: some people make pictures concerned only with the mid-tones and look for a paper that gives the maximum differentiation between the middle greys. Others prize rich, deep shadow detail, and yet others make high-key prints where subtle highlight differentiation is all. Each is likely to prefer a different paper and (which is equally important) a different film developed in a different way. All this emphasizes that you should make your choice based on what you want to achieve.

In practice, there are normally many ways of achieving the same goal, with different combinations of film, exposure, paper, developer and contrast, so the only really useful advice we can offer here is not to chop and change: stick with one paper, almost any paper, and learn to work with that.

Grade 0: very soft

The softest that is ever likely to be needed. Typical ISO(R) 140–160.

Grade 1: soft

Suitable for printing 'plucky' or 'bright' (slightly overdeveloped) negatives. Typical ISO(R) 120–130.

Grade 2: normal (or soft-normal)

Most negatives should print on grade 2. Typical ISO(R) 100–120.

Grade 3: slightly hard or 'vigorous' (or hard-normal)

Adds a bit of 'sparkle' to a flat negative. Typical ISO(R) 90–100.

Grade 4: hard or 'extra-vigorous'

Normally needed only for negatives of very low-contrast subjects, or those that have been underdeveloped. Typical ISO(R) 60–80.

Grade 5: extra-hard

Needed for extremely low-contrast images, or films that are grievously under-exposed or underdeveloped. Typical ISO(R) 40–50.

GRADED AND VARIABLE CONTRAST PAPERS

For many years, papers were manufactured only in discrete grades, and the photographer chose the grade which gave the best results. Skilled photographers adjusted the contrast of their negatives, by varying development time, to suit their favourite paper.

In 1939–40, Ilford devised Multigrade, a variable-contrast (VC) paper, where the contrast could be controlled via the colour of the light used to make the enlargement. At first, VC paper was much inferior to graded, with a limited contrast range and a poor maximum black, but by the mid-1980s there was nothing to choose between the best VC papers (especially Multigrade) and graded papers. ('Multigrade' is often used as a generic term for VC papers, despite being an Ilford trade mark.)

The great advantage of Multigrade and other VC papers is that you can match the grade of the paper exactly to the contrast of the negative, whereas with graded papers, you sometimes find a negative that is a little too contrasty on (say) grade 3, but lacks 'sparkle' on grade 2. With Multigrade there are filters for half-grades as well, so you can get grade 2½ to solve this problem. With a VC head or a colour

head, you can dial in different amounts of yellow or magenta light to get any fractional grade you want: 2.3, say, or 2.7.

The only reasons to use graded papers today are if you particularly like a paper that is not available in VC, or if you need extreme contrast: to this day, a grade 5 graded paper is likely to prove harder than a VC paper at grade 5. There may be older photographers who still decry VC papers, but the odds are that they are remembering the past, not describing the present, possibly because they don't know about it.

HOW VARIABLE-CONTRAST PAPERS WORK

VC papers have two emulsions: one is low in contrast and sensitive to green light, while the other is high in contrast and sensitive to blue. Yellow filtration blocks blue light, so the low-contrast (green-sensitive) emulsion effectively receives more exposure. Magenta filtration blocks green light, so the high-contrast (blue-sensitive) emulsion receives more exposure. By varying the levels of yellow and magenta filtration (or blue and green light), a wide range of contrast grades can be obtained (see page 50).

MULTIGRADE FILTERS AND COLD-CATHODE HEADS

Some enlargers use 'cold-cathode' heads, a similar technology to fluorescent lights. These heads are superb with graded papers, where you don't need filters, but most of them produce a lot of blue light, and the spectrum of light they produce is not continuous. As a result, only a limited range of contrasts is available using filters, and the contrast obtained will not normally match the grade indicated by the filter. There are variable-contrast cold-cathode heads, using two tubes of different colours, but they are very expensive.

▲ *Multigrade filters*

Multigrade filters allow the selection of half grades, with constant exposure times up to grade 4; grade 5 may require double the exposure for grade 3½. There are 12 filters in a set: 00, 0, ½, 1, then half grades to 4½ and 5. The deep red filter, supplied with the Multigrade set, is 'safe' and will not expose the paper: it is used for positioning the paper, especially when making combination prints (see page 82).

COLOUR-HEAD SETTINGS FOR MULTIGRADE

A dial-in Multigrade head is much easier to use than a colour head, but by varying the proportions of magenta and yellow light with a colour head, you can dial in any contrast grade you like. There are, however, three things you need to know.

First, papers from different manufacturers have different contrast grades with the same filtration, though most are pretty close to Multigrade and you can always increase or decrease filtration for more or less contrast.

Second, colour-head filtration values are not standardized: there are several 'families', as described on page 125: this is why the table looks so complicated.

Third, there are two ways to filter. One uses just yellow or just magenta filtration. This means shorter exposure times, but the exposure changes every time the contrast is changed. The other uses different balances of yellow and magenta filtration. This gives constant exposure times, but means longer exposures. The table given on page 125 uses the latter (constant exposure) approach.

useful tips

TWO-FILTER PRINTING
• If you give two exposures sequentially, one at high contrast and one at low contrast, you can achieve infinite adjustment of contrast from 00 to 5 with only two filters. Many people find this 'split-filter' technique easier, though the same effect can always be achieved with a single setting on a Multigrade head.

▶ *Two grades on one print*
An advantage of VC papers – this is Ilford Multigrade Warmtone – is that you can give the main exposure at one contrast grade (in this case 2½) and then burn in extra detail (see page 72) at another contrast grade: here, grade 2 for the contrasty steps at the front.

▶ *Multigrade heads*
Multigrade heads allow you to dial in the requisite paper grade, usually with constant exposure times

◀ *Colour heads*
With colour heads, you can control the colour of the light to give different contrast grades. More yellow gives a softer grade: more magenta gives more contrast.

FB/RC COLOURS AND SURFACES

Most photographic paper used today is coated with a polyethylene (polythene) resin, hence 'RC' (resin coated). It is, however, still possible to buy 'fibre-based' (FB) paper without the resin coating. Many people prefer the look and (especially) the feel of FB, which is available in 'single weight' (thin) and 'double weight' (thick). Untoned FB may also last better on display than untoned RC, but this is by no means certain, and there seems to be no advantage either way if the prints are dark-stored or toned.

FB paper is also known as 'baryta' or 'baryt' paper, because this is what is used to create the bright white background, while RC is also known as PE, from 'polyethylene'.

RC is much tougher than FB, especially when wet. It washes much faster: five minutes or less, instead of 30 minutes or more. And it dries much faster: with a warm-air dryer, in two or three minutes. Despite the fulminations of older photographers, the best RC also delivers excellent quality. If the prints are mounted behind glass, it is impossible to tell whether RC or FB has been used. Until the 1980s, RC papers tended to have an unpleasant, 'milky' look to them, but they are far better now. The vast majority of the prints in this book were made on Ilford Multigrade Warmtone RC, which we regard as the best general-purpose paper on the market.

We have assumed that you will use RC, simply on the grounds of convenience. If you want to switch to FB for 'fine' prints, you will need to handle it more carefully to avoid tearing or creasing, and washing takes longer – though to speed up washing, you can use a wash aid (see page 58).

PAPER COLOUR AND TEXTURE

Today, most papers have a fairly neutral, bright white base, though a few have warmer, slightly creamier base tones: Ilford Multigrade Warmtone, for example. Old photographers sometimes bemoan the passing of 'ivory' and 'cream' and other base colours from the past, though a little fabric dye (or even cold tea) will stain the paper as needed.

useful tips

• For big display prints, glossy paper shows up mounting flaws mercilessly and catches reflections from lights and windows all over the place. A matt or textured paper is much easier.

► *Warm tone*

Some monochrome papers are fairly neutral; some tend towards a bluish ('cool') image tone; and some tend towards a brownish ('warm') tone. These differences are not great, are most apparent under daylight, rather than artificial light, and can be affected by choice of developer (see pages 56–57).

Likewise, there are fewer alternatives to smooth, glossy paper than there used to be – and the names that are used are mightily confusing: 'pearl' and 'lustre' and 'semi-matt' and 'tapestry'. The only thing you can do is to see if you like them. It is next to impossible to convey the effects of the various surfaces in reproduction, though they very definitely have their individual charms when seen 'for real'. Some are available only in FB; some only in RC; and some in both.

DRYING AND SURFACE TEXTURE

RC glossy dries slightly shinier when heat-dried (with a warm-air blower) than when plain air-dried, but FB gloss can vary widely. 'Glossy unglazed' is somewhat more matt than RC glossy, but 'glossy glazed' (where the paper is squeegeed onto glass or a polished metal sheet; see page 61) gives a glass-like surface.

▲ *Warm-toned paper after toning*

Differences in image tone after plain development are much smaller than differences in image tone after toning, but you should not assume that you can use just any old paper and change the colour with toners. Different papers take toners very differently, with warm-toned papers normally exhibiting significantly greater colour shifts. If you plan to tone the image, you should therefore choose a paper that you know from experience (or reputation) will react well to the toning regime you have in mind. This is Ilford Multigrade Warmtone in Paterson Sepia toner.

DRY-DOWN

As a print dries, it loses 'sparkle' and goes darker: this is called 'dry-down'. To make the best final dry print, either dry test strips or work prints (see page 62) before examining them or give a tiny bit less exposure, about five per cent or one second in 20. There is not much you can do about the slight loss of 'sparkle'.

▶ *Cool tone*

The difference between the two prints opposite and right should be just about visible in reproduction: the one opposite was made on Ilford Multigrade RC Warm Tone, and the one on the right was made on Ilford Multigrade RC Cool Tone.

PAPER CHEMISTRY

The chemical baths used for paper are exactly the same in function as those used for film (see pages 14–15): developer, short stop (optional) and fixer. The formulations normally differ, however, and so may the dilution of the fixer. As with film chemistry, liquid concentrates are more convenient and pose less of a health risk.

The main choices in developer are between warm-tone and cool-tone, and rapid-action. As their names suggest, warm-tone developers give a warmer (brownish) tone, cool-tone developers give a cooler (bluish) tone, and rapid-action developers are normally used hot and strong to give extra-rapid development.

You can also buy developers which give a slight increase in contrast, or a significant decrease in contrast. If you are using VC papers, there is not much advantage in this, but with graded papers, it does allow you to get 'intermediate' grades. An old trick is to have two developer baths, one high-contrast and one low-contrast, and to develop the paper for part of the time in one, and part in the other (normally low-contrast first). Tetenal's Dokulith and Centrobrom are a classic off-the-shelf pair for this trick.

The short stop is often used at about half the concentration that is used for film, and fixer may be used at the same strength as for film, or weaker. At film strength, one part to three for Paterson Acufix, it will normally fix the paper in about 30 seconds, while at a greater dilution

fixing times are lengthened: with Acufix one part to seven, they are doubled. The advantage of the lower concentration is economy: regardless of concentration, the capacity of a fixer bath for paper is pretty much constant, because it is limited by a build-up of dissolved silver. It is about 40 20 x 25-cm (8 x 10-in) prints per 1 l (36 fl oz) for FB and 60 to 80 sheets for RC.

TIME AND TEMPERATURE

Below about 18°C (65°F), development becomes very slow. In a cold darkroom, a tray warmer may be all but essential. In the other direction, very high processing temperatures can be used with most modern papers and developers, as high as 38°C (100°F), if you are using a Nova tank and can sustain these temperatures. Warnings in old books about softening of the emulsion and special tropical developers can safely be disregarded.

The exact time for development depends on the temperature and on the developer formulation, and to some extent on the paper: paper that has been stored for a long time will require longer development than fresh paper. A rapid developer at 38°C (100°F), with fresh paper, may develop to finality in 15 to 20 seconds; a slow developer, with old paper, in a cold room, may take five minutes or more. A fair average figure at 20°C (68°F) is 60 to 90 seconds.

▶ **'Snatched' print**
This print was over-exposed and then 'snatched' (taken out of the developer early) in order to stop it going too dark. The faults are clearly visible: muddy tones and poor maximum black.

Flat white ———

Muddy greys ———

Poor maximum black ———

▲ *Correctly exposed print*

Remaking the print at the correct exposure time is the only way to get a good result. A sheet of paper doesn't cost much, and it only takes a few minutes to make something you can be proud of. The differences are most apparent in the trunk of the tree on the right, and the differentiation of the roots in the middle and the leaf on the right.

Dense maximum black

Increased tonal contrast

'Sparkling' whites

useful tips

TWIN FIXING BATHS

A technique used by many photographers, for both economy and archival permanence, is twin fixing baths. Fix for half the recommended time in each bath. When the recommended limit has been reached in the first bath, discard it and replace it with the second bath, which is replaced with a fresh bath. Grievous overfixing (for at least two or three times longer than the maximum recommended) may result in loss of highlight detail and inferior tonality.

DEVELOPMENT BY INSPECTION

Although people say that prints are developed 'by inspection', this is only half right: the only inspection that should actually be needed is to see if they are fully developed. With a Nova tank (see page 22), you can inspect the print from time to time, but you are effectively developing by the same time-and-temperature method as for films: the only difference is that the time must be long enough for the print to be fully developed at the temperature in use. Beginners try to save over-exposed prints by snatching them out of the developer before they darken too far, but this is a false economy: at best you will get a poor maximum black, and at worst you will get streaky, uneven development as well. It is a much better idea to remake the print with less exposure.

THE PROCESSING SEQUENCE

Just as the chemistry is similar for both paper and film, so is the processing sequence: developer, short stop (optional), fixer – but the physical handling of the paper is obviously different. You are working by safelight, so you can see what you are doing, and tongs are advisable for moving the print from one tray to the next. Use colour-coded trays and tongs to minimize the risk of contamination; keep a jug of water handy to rinse the developer tongs if you inadvertently get them into the fixer.

Many traditionalist photographers like to dabble their fingers in the developer, but this a good route both to cross-contamination and (if you are unlucky) to painful dermatitis.

 ## processing the print

The sequence of exposing and making a test strip is given on pages 62–63, and logically, this section might be expected to come after that; but as you have to know how to process a test strip before you can make one, it seemed to make sense to do it this way around.

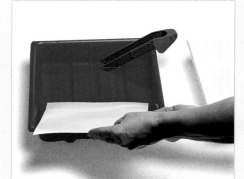

1 Lift the end of the tray nearest you, and slip the print into the developer. Slide the paper forward, while allowing the developer to flow back over the print.

2 Once the print is submerged, rock the tray gently. A low wave should travel across the surface of the print about once a second. After 10 or 20 seconds, an image should start to appear.

3 When the print is fully developed – i.e. when no more density is building in the highlight areas – use the tongs to grip it by the corner. Be firm but gentle, to avoid scratching the surface. Hold the print up and let it drain for a few seconds, until the developer is just dripping gently off instead of flowing off.

4 Drop the print into the short stop, taking care not to contaminate the developer tongs, and rock for about 30 seconds. Remove with the short stop/fixer tongs; drain as before; and place the print in the fixer for the recommended time (60 seconds with Acufix one part to seven).

useful tip

WASH AID

To save time and water when washing FB, wash for two minutes; transfer to wash aid (in a tray, or in a washer slot) for the time recommended (typically around 10 minutes); then wash for 10 more minutes. Do not wash in the same tray (or slot) as prints undergoing their first wash.

5 At the end of the recommended fixing time, remove the print from the fixer with the fixer tongs; drain; and, holding a tray or saucer under the corner to catch any further drips, transfer it to the washer. Wash for two minutes (RC), 30 minutes (FB single weight) or 60 minutes (FB double weight). Remember that you must count from the time that the last print went into the washer.

6 The final print has a good range of tones, including detail in the shadow on the right of the door and texture in the bright remnants of whitewashed stucco that still cling to the wall.

DRYING, GLAZING AND FLATTENING PRINTS

Drying prints is another of those areas which often receives short shrift in books and magazines – but there are quite a few options, at widely differing prices.

All prints lose contrast and increase in density as they 'dry down', and it is therefore a good idea to dry your test strips (see page 62) before you decide on your final exposure and paper grade. After a brief wash, both RC and FB papers can be rapid-dried with a hair dryer.

The important thing with all drying is to make sure that the print is well washed. If it is not, it will eventually develop stains, and it may contaminate the surface on which it is dried. For a test strip, dried with a hair dryer while resting on a paper towel, this won't matter. For a final print, it may.

After you have made and washed a print, transfer it to a final bath containing wetting agent made up to the manufacturer's recommended strength. This will promote rapid and even drying of both RC and FB papers. If you live in a very hard-water area, consider making up the final bath with distilled or purified water rather than tap water: it can be reused repeatedly.

STAGE 2: DRYING RC PRINTS

One of the numerous advantages of RC paper is that it is much quicker and easier to dry than FB.

STAGE 1: SQUEEGEEING

The first thing, whatever paper you use, is to remove as much water as possible, for faster drying without marks.

◀ The first stage
What we normally do after the final rinse in wetting agent is to lay the paper against a sheet of Perspex (or Lucite or glass) and remove all surface water with a squeegee; Paterson's print squeegee can be used with smaller prints. The next step depends on whether we are drying RC or FB paper.

▲ *Option 1*
The quickest and most convenient way to dry RC prints is in an RC dryer like this one from Nova. Unfortunately, it is also one of the most expensive ways – but the print can be dry in two or three minutes. Turning off the heater and running the fan only for the last minute or so will reduce curling.

▲ *Option 2*
If an RC drier is too expensive or too inconvenient (they are pretty bulky), a drying rack like this one from Paterson is ideal and inexpensive. Both RC and FB prints can be dried on one of these or on a 'clothes line', but FB (especially single weight) may curl. If the emulsions of two damp prints touch, they are likely to weld together inseparably.

STAGE 2: DRYING FB PRINTS

The biggest single problem with FB prints is persuading them to dry flat, but another important consideration is avoiding contamination.

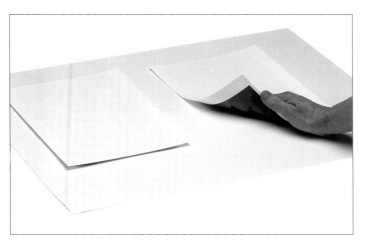

▲ *Option 1*

A traditional way to dry FB prints is on, or between, blotters. Drying them in a stack keeps them admirably flat, but prints may need to be dried sequentially in two or three stacks of dry blotters. The blotters themselves are dried in an airing cupboard or somewhere similar. The final drying of the print can be face-down on the blotter, as shown here.

▲ *Option 2*

Another traditional way to dry FB prints is with a flat-bed dryer like this one from Nova. For an unglazed finish, the print is simply held against the dryer surface with the emulsion against the fabric 'blanket'. If there is any possibility that the blanket has been contaminated by being used to dry poorly washed prints, wash it thoroughly or replace it. Do not dry RC prints this way, as they may melt onto the dryer.

useful tip

• If you are glazing FB prints, clean either the glass or the glazing plates with a non-abrasive cleaner, and wash generously, to get the best possible glaze and to minimize sticking. If prints do stick, your only hope is to soak them off.

▲ *Option 3*

For a glazed finish, FB prints are first soaked in a glazing solution (Tetenal makes one), then squeegeed into close contact with a sheet of glass and left to dry until they fall off of their own accord. Alternatively, they can be squeegeed onto a thin, flexible, mirror-polished 'glazing plate' or 'ferrotype plate' that can then be put in a flat-bed dryer, print uppermost. Again, do not try to glaze RC prints this way.

FLATTENING PRINTS

The best way to flatten curly prints is by leaving them overnight (or longer) under a stack of heavy books, or by flattening them in a dry-mounting press (see page 100). 'Flattening agents' allow the print to dry flat, but we have never found them very satisfactory: the print feels limp and clammy, and smells funny too. The brave may try to flatten prints by dragging them under a ruler, against the curve, or over the edge of a table.

TEST STRIPS AND WORK PRINTS

Test strips enable you to determine the best exposure and contrast grade for printing from a given negative, without using numerous whole sheets of paper. Once you have decided these, you make a work print, which is a straight print of the entire negative. Sometimes, especially for record shots, a work print is all you will need: it is your final print.

The work print is only a stepping stone. From it, you can gauge whether the picture will look better cropped (see page 70), dodged or burned (see page 72) or subjected to other manipulations. Even if you are going to make a big exhibition print such as 30 x 40 cm (12 x 16 in), you can learn a great deal from an 20 x 25 cm (8 x 10-in) work print.

test strips for exposure

The cheapest way to make test strips is with a piece of black card, and half a sheet or even a quarter sheet of 20 x 25 cm (8 x 10-in) paper; there is no need to use a whole sheet. First, you make a test strip for exposure; then, when you are confident that you have approximately the right exposure, you make another for contrast. With more experience, you will soon be able to judge both exposure and contrast simultaneously.

◄ *2 Set the lens to f/5.6 and the contrast grade to two (or use a grade two filter). These middle-of-the-road settings should give a satisfactory starting point with most negatives. With the entire paper uncovered, expose for two seconds. Now cover one-fifth of the paper, and give two more seconds. Repeat, covering another fifth of the paper each time. Give four seconds for the third exposure, eight for the fourth and 16 for the fifth.*

◄ *3 Develop the test strip. The full exposure sequence will be 2–4–8–16–32 sec. Select the best exposure; go 'between strips if necessary (e.g. use 12 seconds if eight is too light and 16 is too dark). If all the segments are too dark, repeat the test at f/11.*

▲ *1 For your first attempt, choose a sharp negative with a good tonal range, and detail in both the shadows and the highlights. Set the enlarger to give an 'all in' print (the whole negative) on an 20 x 25 cm (8 x 10-in) sheet of paper, and focus.*

2 sec   4 sec   8 sec   16 sec   32 sec

test strips for contrast

Once you have your 'best guess' for exposure, you can fine-tune contrast. If the best exposed area of the test strip is too harsh and contrasty, try a grade softer, for example. grade 1 instead of grade 2. If it looks flat and grey, try a grade harder, for example. grade 3. After this test, you may even need to go softer or harder again, to grade 0 or 4. Test an area of the print with a good range of tones.

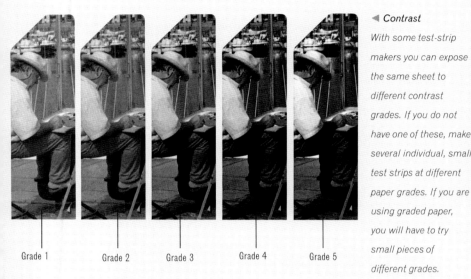

Grade 1 Grade 2 Grade 3 Grade 4 Grade 5

◀ *Contrast*

With some test-strip makers you can expose the same sheet to different contrast grades. If you do not have one of these, make several individual, small test strips at different paper grades. If you are using graded paper, you will have to try small pieces of different grades.

▲ *The work print*

Make a print using the exposure and contrast grade indicated by the test strips. This is a 'work print'.

TEST STRIP MAKERS

Over the years, numerous test strip makers have been introduced, and have fallen by the wayside. They fall into two groups: those where you make a series of exposures side by side, using a large area of the negative (or even all of it), and those where you make a series of exposures of the same small area of the negative, moving the paper between each exposure.

▶ *Nova test strip maker*

The Nova step-and-repeat test strip maker is of the second type. You move a fresh area of a single piece of paper into the window for each exposure, so you are always comparing the same part of the print.

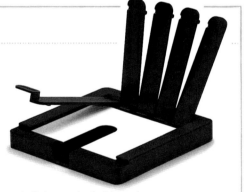

▲ *Paterson test strip maker*

The Paterson test strip maker is of the first type: the 'fingers' effectively mechanize the process described above. Close them one after the other to make the test strip.

USEFUL TIPS

• When making test strips and work prints, take care to avoid cross-contaminating the solutions with the tongs.

• Remember that if you are using a colour head, you may need to adjust the exposure for each contrast grade.

• Many variable-contrast papers require twice as much exposure at grade 5 as at other grades.

CONTACT SHEETS

Contact prints are entirely separate from test strips, but they can serve the same purpose to a considerable extent, as they can help you to judge both the likely exposure and likely contrast grade needed for a particular picture – especially if you have printed anything else from the same film, as you can then compare the contact prints of both images for contrast and exposure.

Although it is entirely possible to make contact prints using only a sheet of glass, it is much more convenient either to use a purpose-made contact printer, such as the Paterson illustrated here, or to print the negatives in their sleeves on a larger sheet of paper. Transparent sleeves, such as the Print File type illustrated here, are essential for the latter, as well as offering superior protection.

Using a soft grade of paper will enable you to see all of the detail on all but the most contrasty negatives, and making two (or even three) sheets at different exposures will enable you to see all the detail, even in negatives that have been over- or under-exposed.

making a contact sheet

Making contact sheets is tedious work – there is no doubt about it. Most photographers (including ourselves) would rather skip the preliminaries and get down to the business of printing final images straight away, so all too often contacts just don't get made.

However, it is much easier to judge your pictures from contacts than in the form of negatives, and when we don't make contacts, we tend to regret not having done so.

1 Place the negatives in the slots of the contact printer. This model holds seven strips of six exposures on 35mm for contact printing on 24 x 30-cm (9½ x 12-in) paper. A smaller model allows six strips of six exposures to be printed on 20 x 25-cm (8 x 10 in) paper: easier to find, but cramped, and a nuisance if you have 37 exposures.

2 Working under a safelight, insert a sheet of soft (grade 1) paper into the printing frame and place it on the enlarger baseboard. With a 50mm lens at f/8, 40 cm (16 in) above the baseboard, expose for 10 seconds. Develop the contact sheet, and alter the exposure (though not the contrast) as necessary to get the majority of negatives well exposed.

3 After the contact print is dry use a magnifying glass and a Chinagraph or similar wax-pencil to mark up the images for enlarging. If need be, put another sheet in and print a second sheet to get detail in over- or under-exposed negatives.

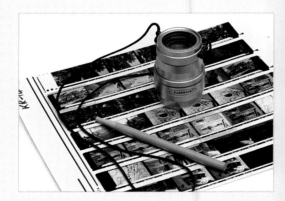

ELECTRONIC 'CONTACT SHEETS'

If you have a scanner that can handle transparencies, you can scan your negatives in batches and either examine them on screen or print them out same-size (like traditional contacts), enlarged or even reduced. You can also modify individual frames, lightening or darkening them, or altering contrast, to make the contact sheet easier to read.

useful tip
• It is sad but true that an image which looks really good as a negative can be disappointing as a print. Often this is because the dark edge of the negative defines the image: when it is printed, the dark areas print as light, and the image 'leaks away' at the edges. Printing with a black border, or with a filed-out negative carrier (see pages 74 and 78), can sometimes ameliorate this problem.

▶ *Resolution*

Scanning at 300 dpi will give more than enough resolution for on-screen viewing and is adequate for ink-jet print-outs of individual frames at about 5 x 7 cm (2 x 3 in); file sizes are around 30 Mb (uncompressed) – which still means one can fit 20 or more 'contact sheets' onto a single 650 Mb CD-ROM. This is from a 300-dpi scan, without taking the negatives out of the file sleeve: this does nothing for sharpness, but is much more convenient.

▶ *Using a scanner*

Most A4 scanners can handle 20 x 25-cm (8 x 10-in) transparencies, so it is just possible to get six strips of six exposures on 35mm onto the scanner area. Alternatively, and rather more easily, you can leave the negatives in their sleeve (as here) and make two scans, each of around half the negatives. For maximum convenience, stitch the two together electronically to give a single file.

TROUBLESHOOTING PRINTS

It is quite difficult (though far from impossible) to fail to get an image altogether on a print. Far likelier are prints that are made on the wrong grade of paper; or over- or under-exposed; or underdeveloped (you are likely to get bored long before you can overdevelop a print); or badly fixed or washed.

Remember, though, that printing is very much a question of taste. A print that looks 'rich' to one photographer will merely look dark and muddy to another, while a print which is 'bright' (or even 'sparkling') to one will look too contrasty to another. The only way to learn to judge print quality in your own work, as well as deciding what sort of print you like, is by looking at high-quality prints in exhibitions. Even the best photomechanical reproductions cannot do justice to a first-class original print.

▶ *Bad blacks*

If you never get a good black, no matter how long you develop the print, then the problem is likely to be under-exposure, though it may also be exhausted or very cold developer.

Another recipe for this common type of problem is that beginners may attempt to 'snatch' an overexposed print out of the developer before it is fully developed.
Remedy: Don't snatch.

▲ *Flat look*

A too-soft grade of paper can give a full range of tones, from white to a good black, and still look 'flat'.
Remedy: Remake the print on harder paper.

◀ *Stains*

Stains are almost invariably due to poor fixing or poor washing, or both. Poor fixing may be a result of fixing for too short a time, or overusing fixer; poor washing may be a result of fixing for too short a time, or of prints sticking together when being washed.
Remedy: Fix for the recommended time; don't overuse the fixer; wash for the recommended time.

◀ *Poor mid-tones*

A too-hard grade of paper will give what used to be called a 'soot-and-whitewash' print: plenty of blacks and whites, but a poor range of mid-tones.
Remedy: Remake the print on softer paper.

▲ Bad borders

It is horribly easy to put the paper in the easel incorrectly, or to set the borders incorrectly, or to get a sliver of light from just outside the edge of the negative which records as a pure black. Sometimes you can do all three! If you are lucky, you can crop the borders, but as a general rule, it's best not to try to kid yourself.

Remedy: Remake the print.

▲ Mirror image

If the print is a mirror image, but otherwise technically good, the chances are that the negative is reversed in the enlarger carrier.

Remedy: It should be shiny-side up, with the emulsion facing down towards the paper. The emulsion side is less shiny than the non-emulsion side, though some films are shinier than others.

▲ Dirty condition

This negative was processed by an allegedly 'professional' lab, which left us with the filthiest negatives we have ever seen. Then they had the nerve to say, 'Well, we'd just cleaned the machine.' They had apparently stirred up all the sludge and debris when they poured in the new chemistry – and it ended up on our negatives.

Remedy: For this film, a lot of work. For the next film, another lab.

▲ Mirror image plus loss of sharpness

If the print is not only a mirror image, but also fuzzy and flat, and quite possibly under-exposed as well, you may well have put the paper in the enlarging easel the wrong way up. This is particularly easy with matt, fibre-based paper.

Remedy: Put the paper in the right way up!

ADVANCED PRINTING

Most advanced-printing techniques are easy enough: the only real difficulty lies in using them aggressively enough to get the desired effect, without making them too obvious. Novices tend to be timorous, creating a picture that is too close to the work print. Alternatively, they may leave traces of their handiwork, with glowing halos at the edge of dodged or burned areas and unnatural-looking transition areas between different parts of the image. The only way around this is practice!

It is possible to be too critical, too analytical. A photographic print should be like a theatrical performance. You should 'suspend disbelief' and accept that the print is in one sense unreal, and in another, more real than reality. Even a great print may wilt in the glare of technical analysis; but if only the technique hits you in the face, then the image has failed as a picture.

CROPPING

Purely technically, it is a good idea to avoid cropping whenever possible. The more of the negative you use, the less the degree of magnification, and the higher the quality; but often, practical or aesthetic considerations overrule technical ideals.

In the real world, after all, you sometimes have the wrong lens on the camera; or can't get close enough; or fail to notice something off to one side of the picture; or tilt the camera slightly; or take pictures which do not 'want' to be the same shape as the negative. There is also the dilemma of standard paper sizes that do not always match standard film sizes: if you want to print 35mm on 20 x 25-cm (8 x 10-in) paper, for example, you have the choice of 'wasting' some of the paper area by printing 'all-in', or throwing away some of the information on the long dimension of the negative.

Some people believe that it shows 'integrity' always to print everything 'all-in', without cropping, but all that this shows is that they are better at believing than at thinking. Who, after all, decided which lens to use; where to stand; and when to press the shutter release? How does cropping differ from this?

Sometimes, the necessary crop is so obvious that you can see it on the contact print, or when the negative is projected onto the enlarger baseboard, but cropping on the baseboard is something you should undertake with caution because it is hard to judge the compositional 'weight' of tonal masses when they are in negative.

Remember that you are not restricted to conventional paper sizes. If a picture works better as a long, thin crop, or if a rectangular picture looks better square, then just reset the blades of your enlarging easel and print that way!

▶ *Cropping to change format*

This is a classic 'happy snap' taken from too far away, and with the camera held horizontally (landscape format). The cropped version removes all the extraneous background, strengthens the composition, and (in the process) changes it from landscape to portrait format (vertical).

▲ *The work print*

As a general rule, the work print should be 'all-in', so that you can judge the ideal crop, preferably using black-card L-brackets as illustrated. Just slide them around until you get a composition you like – and remember, there may be two (or more) pictures 'hiding' inside a single negative.

useful tips

• If you have access to a computer and scanner, try cropping on screen. Just scan in the print, then view different areas of the print on the monitor screen. This has the advantage that instead of seeing the print smaller and smaller as you crop it, you can always blow it up to a size that fills your screen.

• Remember that on-screen resolution flatters a print: if you tried to blow a small part of a negative up to the size of a 17-inch monitor, the quality of the resulting print will be disappointing.

► Cropping to level the viewpoint

If you tilt the camera to get rid of an uninteresting foreground, you get a 'falling-over-backwards' effect. To avoid this, hold the camera level (near right) and crop out the unnecessary foreground (far right).

◄ Cropping to make a panorama

There is nothing sacred about the shape of any given format, and you should not hesitate to crop if, by doing so, you can get a picture that is a more pleasing or striking shape, like this panorama.

► Two in one

The 'all-in' picture not only has two centres of interest: it also exhibits two very different sets of lighting conditions, which really demand different paper grades. One of the two 'half prints' is on grade $2\frac{1}{2}$ and the other on grade 3, and the exposures are different. The bucket in the middle is in both pictures.

DODGING AND BURNING

In the work print, some areas may be too dark, while others are too light. But if the detail is there on the negative, it can be captured on the print by local 'burning' – giving more exposure, to darken part of the print – or 'dodging', holding back light for part of the exposure, to make it lighter. As well as being used remedially, both may also be used creatively, to bring the picture closer to what the photographer wants.

Deciding where and how much to burn or dodge is a matter of experience, though the test strip (see page 62) can give you a good guide to the amount of exposure needed for different areas of the print.

Generally, you need to burn for at least 50 per cent longer than the base exposure in order to make a perceptible difference; 100 to 200 per cent is commonplace; and 400 to 500 per cent (4x–5x) is not unknown.

Dodging is generally more subtle than burning: it is typically done for anything from 10 to 50 per cent of the main exposure. If you are too heavy-handed, it will look obvious and unnatural, but if you are too faint-hearted, it will not show. The differences should be just about visible in these small reproductions, but they are much clearer in original prints, especially big ones.

burning in a sky

Perhaps the most common application of burning is to darken a flat or dull sky. In this picture, the horizon is straight, so it is easy: for more complicated skylines, you may need to cut away part of the edge of a piece of card, or tape bits on.

1 The test strip indicated that the foreground looked best at 15 seconds, while the sky looked better at 30; the work print was made for the foreground: 15 seconds at grade 2.

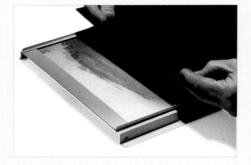

2 After giving the initial 15 seconds, the sky is 'burned in' for a further 15 seconds, using a piece of cardboard to shield the rest of the scene. Keep the cardboard moving either side of the horizon, a total movement of about 1 cm (½ in) during the exposure, to avoid a harsh, clear line.

3 With the extra exposure, the sky is darker and more dramatic. For still greater drama, change filtration for printing the sky: if the overall exposure is at grade 2, switch to grade 4 (much harder) for the sky.

dodging and burning details

As already indicated, dodging and burning should not normally be obvious; the final print should look entirely natural. Light halos around dodged areas, and dark shadows beside burned areas, are generally a sign of unsuccessful work, though some photographers seem not to mind, and almost make a feature of their dodging and burning. In the end, this is very much a matter of personal preference and style.

1 'Mark up' the work print to remind yourself what needs doing. The sunlit water and rocks, lower left, are turned out to white; the trunk of the tree is blocked up to black; and the print 'leaks out' of the corners which are too light. Darkening the corners is often a good way to concentrate attention on the principal subject, and to unify the composition.

2 During the main exposure, a dodging wand is used to 'hold back' the tree trunk. Use a piece of wire or thin plastic for the handle, and tip it with a small piece of cardboard cut or torn to size or (as here) some cotton wool for a very soft edge. It was used for about one-third of the total exposure, moving constantly up and down the trunk.

3 During a second exposure, a card with a hole in it is used to 'burn' the patch of too-bright sunlight for five times as long as the base exposure. The negative clearly held the detail, but was very dense.

useful tips

• Keep the dodging (or burning) tools moving during the exposure, to avoid too clear an edge to your handiwork.

• When burning in a light area, burn into the neighbouring dark area slightly in order to avoid a 'halo' around the subject.

• An enlarger timer makes it easier to give multiple exposures for burning.

4 The photographer's hands can make a useful dodging tool to darken the corners. A piece of card shades the rest of the print, either resting directly on it, or (as here) held above. You can get through quite a lot of thin card or black sugar-paper when you are dodging and burning! Here, the upper right corner was given 100 per cent extra exposure; the upper left corner, 200 per cent extra; and the two lower corners, 300 per cent each.

5 If you did not know what the work print looked like, you could not easily guess that the final print had been dodged or burned at all. All manipulation was done at the same grade (2) because this is easier than constantly changing grades; reduces the risk of knocking either the enlarger or the easel between exposures; and often (though not always) looks more natural than varying grades.

FILED-OUT NEGATIVE CARRIERS

Many negative carriers are slightly smaller than the actual 35mm image, so some photographers file out their negative carriers to allow genuinely 'all-in' printing. They also like the rough edge that this gives them: this technique is particularly popular with those who believe in the 'integrity' of printing 'all-in', without cropping.

Preferably using a spare negative carrier or (as here) a replaceable carrier mask, scribe all around the mask to give an area approximately 25 x 38 mm (1 x 1½ in), and file out to the scribed lines with a ward file. Smooth the edges carefully with fine emery cloth, to avoid scratched

negatives, and paint the filed-out edges with matt black to avoid unwanted flare.

Nominal and actual sizes

The nominal image size on 35mm is 24 x 36 mm, but some cameras have a smaller film gate, as little as 23 x 34 mm – about 8 per cent smaller. With others, extreme wide-angle lenses can 'see under' the edge of the film gate, resulting in a negative that can be as much as 25 x 38 mm – about 10 per cent bigger.

Filed and unfiled carriers

The effects of a filed carrier (right) and an unfiled carrier (above) are abundantly clear here. As with so much else in photography, the choice is a question of aesthetics and fashion, not of what is 'correct'.

VIGNETTING

In Queen Victoria's day, and for long afterwards, vignetting was a common way of presenting photographs, especially portraits. Instead of having a hard edge, the image just fades to white or (more rarely) to sepia. Today, the process is so little used that it is often mispronounced as 'vig-netting' instead of the correct 'veen-yetting'. It could, however, hardly be easier. Devotees of vignetting often keep a selection of pre-cut masks in various sizes and shapes, but oval masks are most often useful. Choose a negative with a fair amount of 'land' around the main subject, or the edge of the frame will come in during vignetting.

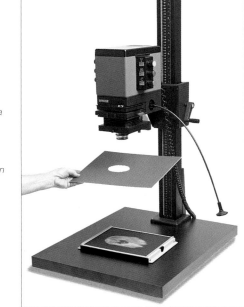

▶ Using the mask
Hold the vignetting mask a hand-span above the paper during the exposure. Keep it moving, in order to soften the edges. Use a rotary motion parallel with the paper, or an up-and-down motion on the lens-paper axis. By varying the distance from the paper, vignettes of different sizes are obtained.

▼ Sepia toning
For a really Victorian effect, sepia-tone the final image (see page 92).

▲ Be bold!
As with everything else in photography, do not be afraid to play with an idea. Does this remind you of an Arab girl in a burqa? Or of a mischievous sparkle in the eyes? (Not that the two are necessarily mutually exclusive, of course...).

▲ Fade to black
For a fade to black, fully expose the main subject. Attach a mask to the end of a piece of wire like a dodging wand (see page 73) and hold it over the main subject while you expose the rest of the paper. Keep the mask moving during exposure, to avoid hard shadows. Extremely generous exposure, as much as four or five stops, may be needed to ensure that light areas at the edge of the picture go completely black. Alternatively, use a second enlarger (see page 77).

SOFT FOCUS

Far and away the best way to get soft-focus (SF) effects is the same way our ancestors did – with contact prints from large negatives made using specialist SF lenses. Modern SF lenses or SF screens are the next best choice, though shooting SF on 35mm is never going to be as satisfactory as shooting on larger formats.

It is, however, possible to get SF effects at the enlargement stage, by putting some form of diffuser under the enlarger lens. The effects will vary according to the type of diffuser used and its distance from the lens They will never be the same as you would get at the taking stage, because at the taking stage the highlights spread into the shadows, while at the enlarging stage the shadows spread into the highlights (because, of

course, you are working in negative). The best effects at the enlargement stage are often obtained by using quite a powerful diffuser for only part of the exposure. This superimposes a sharp image on an unsharp one, which is generally more pleasing. Begin with a 50–50 split, and change the proportions for more or less diffusion.

ENLARGER FILTER SYSTEMS

'System' filters for cameras are popular enough, but adapters are available to allow the use of some of these filters (and some made only for enlarging) on enlarger lenses. Soft focus and vignetting (see page 75) are just two possible applications.

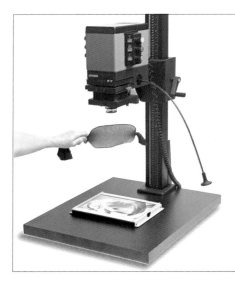

◀ *Getting a soft-focus effect*

Make a frame from wire: a coat-hanger is ideal. Stretch a piece of black muslin or something similar over it – sheer tights work well – and secure it, if necessary, with glue or a few stitches. During the exposure, hold the diffuser about 5 cm (2 in) under the enlarger lens for part of the exposure.

Soft focus   *Hard focus*

useful tips

There are a number of ways of achieving different effects:

• Perforating the diffuser

• Holding the diffuser closer to the paper

• Using different diffuser materials (such as white muslin, which will reduce contrast)

Hard and soft focus

Even at this size, the differences between these two 20 x 25-cm (8 x 10-in) prints of Sophie Muscat-King should be clear: look at the texture of the flying helmet, and the hair.

PRE-FLASHING

Skilled printers use pre-flashing when faced with a difficult negative that looks flat and muddy at a lower contrast grade, but which loses highlight and shadow detail when printed at a higher-contrast grade. It works because all materials have an exposure 'threshold'. Any exposure lower than this will produce no image. Pre-flashing uses a short pre-exposure to overcome this 'inertia', so that any subsequent exposure will be immediately effective. Because it relies on quantum electronic effects, pre-flashing cannot be done at the time of manufacture: a pre-flashed sheet of paper will, after a while, revert to its original inertia. Some photographers use a cheap old enlarger with a junk lens, just for pre-flashing, alongside their main working enlarger.

HOW TO PRE-FLASH

Determine the necessary pre-flash exposure by making a test strip with no negative in the carrier, the lens stopped down to f/8 and the head well up the column. You want to discover the longest exposure that will not give any tone at all in the print. If you have a quarter-stop timer, use that. Otherwise, the quarter-stop exposure sequence (in seconds) is 1–1. 2–1. 4–1. 7–2–2. 4–2. 8–3. 4–4–4. 8–5. 6–6. 8–8–9. 6–11–13–16–19–22. Try the first five or six on your first test strip: if that does not give you a tone, continue where you left off. Dry the test strip before you judge the faintest area with tone (see page 60).

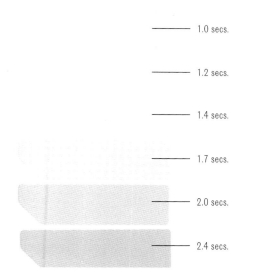

——— 1.0 secs.

——— 1.2 secs.

——— 1.4 secs.

——— 1.7 secs.

——— 2.0 secs.

——— 2.4 secs.

▲ *Pre-flash test*

Here, the 1.2-seconds pre-flash was the last not to give a detectable tone, so the exposure below this is one second. Pre-flash the entire sheet of paper on which you are going to make your print at one second.

▶ *Pre-flash and no flash*

Using the same exposure you used for your unsuccessful prints, print on the pre-flashed sheet, using the higher-contrast grade in this case, grade 3. Process normally. Here, one half of the paper was pre-flashed, and the other was not, to show the difference as clearly as possible. The real difference is in the lightest highlights, which are 'blown' on the non-flashed side, but fully textured on the pre-flashed side.

BORDERS AND PIN LINES

Some photographers make only borderless prints, or trim the borders off their prints so that they appear borderless. Others use only a standardized border width, traditionally 0.9 or 1 cm ($\frac{5}{16}$ or $\frac{3}{8}$ in) or for small prints and 2 or 2.5 cm ($\frac{3}{4}$ or 1 in) for larger prints. Many believe that the bottom border should be wider than the other three borders – and then there are pin lines, and the kind of 'all-in' lines produced by filed-out carriers (see page 74) or replicated with masks (see opposite). A few photographers even use black borders. Which is best? No-one can answer this for you, but there is no doubt that some types of border are much easier to make than others.

▶ **Single-format easel**

Single-format easels,
like this one from
Paterson, are quick
and easy to use and
give a white border of
fixed width.

◀ **Two-blade easel**

Two-blade easels, like
this (very old) Kayfro,
typically allow the
creation of white
borders of variable
width, equal or unequal,
on all four sides.

▲ **Four-blade easel**

Four-blade easels, like this one from RR Beard, allow borders of almost any
size on all four sides – a 10 x 12.5-cm (4 x 5-in) print in the middle of a sheet of
30 x 40-cm (12 x 16-in) paper, if you like – but take longer to set up for different
paper sizes and border widths. Once they are set up, they are as quick to use
as two-blade easels.

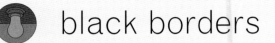

black borders

The easiest way to create a black border is with the Borderline easel, although it is entirely possible to make up something similar using black cardboard. The effect can be somewhat funereal, and you need to choose your subjects carefully.

1 Make initial
exposures using the
Borderline, place the
masking plate, and
turn on the room
lights for 5 or 10
seconds to fog two
edges of the border.
Turn them off;
remove the masking
plate; turn the paper
180°; replace the
masking plate; and
fog the other edges.

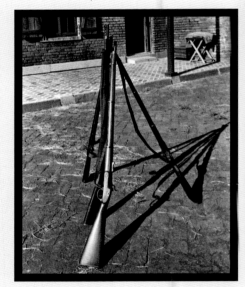

2 Develop normally, and you have a print with
black borders. This has to be used with discretion,
because of the funereal effect; here, at a American
Civil War re-enactment site, it seems appropriate
as a memorial to the dead on both sides.

pin lines

Any easel – single-format, two-blade or four-blade – can be used to give a simple pin line, with opposite sides (top and bottom, or left and right) of equal width. A four-blade easel gives a wider choice of options, but involves more work. The first step, with either, is to cut an opaque black mask of exactly the same size as the image area.

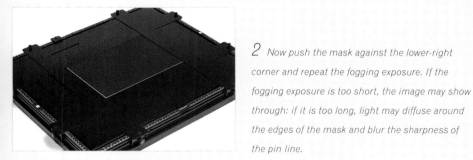

2 Now push the mask against the lower-right corner and repeat the fogging exposure. If the fogging exposure is too short, the image may show through: if it is too long, light may diffuse around the edges of the mask and blur the sharpness of the pin line.

1 With any easel, compose the image so that it is just inside the blades: 0.2–0.4 cm ($^1/_{10}$–$^1/_6$ in) on all sides, depending on the width of the pin line desired. Make the exposure, then drop the mask in, and push it against the upper left hand corner of the frame, so that there is a gap along two edges. Expose generously, typically 3–5 stops more than the base exposure, or use room lights for 5–10 seconds.

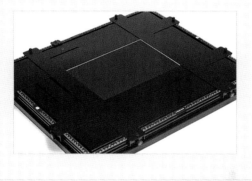

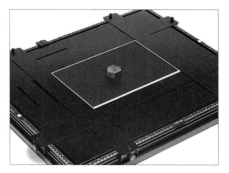

▲ *Pin lines using a four-blade easel*

With a four-blade easel, you can also work as follows. First, set up the image to precisely the size of the mask. Make the exposure. Drop the mask into place and secure it with a weight or magnets. Move the blades outwards to the desired degree: this easel has user pre-set stops to make this easier. You can make pin lines of uneven widths: four at 0.2 cm ($^1/_{10}$ in) and one at 0.3 cm ($^1/_8$ in), say, or whatever is desired. Make the exposure, or use room lights, as with the two-blade, and develop the print.

▶ *Avoiding 'bleed-off'*

Pin lines are particularly useful when there are light areas that might otherwise 'bleed off' the edge of the image, but they can help to emphasize any composition, and they are all but indispensable if you want to print a small image in the centre of a large sheet of paper. This is a protest outside the Russian White House in 1992.

TEXTURE SCREENS AND FRAMES

Both texture screens and frames are high-contrast negatives that are designed to be sandwiched together with an image negative, superimposing their own structure on it. Texture screens come in numerous patterns – photographic grain, etching, craquelure (the pattern that forms on old paintings) and so forth – while frames come in an equal variety of shapes to go around the image.

Slightly different effects are obtainable by placing the effects negative above or below the main image negative, or emulsion-to-emulsion instead of both emulsion down, and different manufacturers' effects negatives can differ quite widely, even when the names are similar or identical. They are available in a range of sizes: almost everyone does 35mm, but roll-film sizes are rather rarer. You can also buy big screens (from Textureffects) that are designed to be sandwiched with the print, rather than with the negative, though these are understandably expensive.

Although they are often illustrated for use with colour, texture screens and frames may well be more effective with black and white.

▲ Using high contrast

With some texture screens you may find that results are more successful with a higher-contrast grade. The straight shot (top) is on grade 3; the 'steel-etch' shot (above) is on grade 5, using a Paterson screen.

◀ Texture screens

Scrupulous cleanliness is essential when sandwiching two negatives together, as there are two more surfaces to gather (and seemingly attract) dust. On the bright side, the broken-up image is usually easier to retouch. These are Paterson's texture screens.

▲ Speckled edges

Frames mask off part of the image, and are easier to illustrate than to describe. The examples shown here are from The FX Files. They can give unique effects, such as 'speckle edge' in this picture of Tsering Youdon at the Taragarh Palace...

▲ Hand-coated paper?

... or even resemble hand-coated paper, as in this picture of Tsering Youdon at the Tibetan Institute for Performing Arts.

► 'Film' edges

... or a print that apparently includes the edge of the film, like this darkroom shot from the Amnye Machen Institute in Dharamsala...

SANDWICH AND COMBINATION PRINTING

Basic 'sandwich' printing has already been described on pages 80–81 in the context of texture screens and frames, and of course just about any two negatives can be combined. Remember, however, that the dark areas of both negatives will predominate, so if you want any dark areas in the final print, you must make sure that the light areas of the two negatives overlap. The effect is quite different from a sequential double exposure, where the light areas in both negatives predominate.

▶ *Separate images*

The original images are of a Confederate war memorial in the Southern United States, and the Virginia Military Institute where so many soldiers on both sides trained. The idea was to show a continuity, the past overshadowing the present as modern cadets commemorate the Battle of Newmarket.

◀ *Sandwiched image*

In the sandwiched image, the memorial is much stronger and the gateway is darker.

▶ *Double exposure*

In the double-exposed image, the memorial is more ghostly and contrast is reduced, but the relative sizes of the two images can be adjusted.

USEFUL TIP

PREPARATORY WORK

• If you consider it would be helpful, sketch both the images you are going to sandwich together onto a sheet of paper placed on on the baseboard (see right).

combination printing

Combination printing is much more versatile than sandwiching. Victorian masters of the art would combine numerous images onto a single print: O.G. Rejlander, in his famous 1857 picture, The Two Ways of Life, used over 30. Most photographers, however, restrict themselves to 'dropping in' skies, if they use the technique at all: it used to be much more popular in the past. Devotees of combination printing tend to have whole libraries of skies.

The sky is completely bald behind this visitor centre at the park commemorating the Battle of Chickamauga in the Southern United States.

This is one of a series of sky negatives shot with combination printing in mind. Next time we shall shoot some in 'portrait' format as well.

1 Size up the first negative up on the enlarger baseboard. Measure the head elevation, or note it from the column.

2 Support a piece of black card above the baseboard on a couple of books, and sketch in the out-of-focus outline of the skyline.

3 Size up the sky negative, and again note the head elevation. A work print makes a useful guide to exactly where you want the clouds to fall – or you can use a sketch of the skyline, from step three above.

4 Cut a pair of masks from the black card, conforming to the skyline. Make separate test strips to determine exposure for the landscape and the sky. Make the first exposure (of the landscape) with the sky mask in place, so only the landscape is recorded.

5 Make the second exposure (of the sky) with the landscape mask in place, so that only the sky records. Some people move the mask during the exposure; others don't – see which works best for you. Dodge or burn as necessary (see page 72) at the same time that you are making the combination print.

In the final print, there is a slight 'halo' beside the right-hand side of the roof: on the left, the sky has been burned into the roof slightly, to make it less obtrusive. Different photographers tend to prefer one approach or the other.

PERSPECTIVE CONTROL

The familiar 'falling-over-backwards' effect, which results from tilting the camera upwards to photograph a tall building, can be corrected to some extent at the enlarging stage. It relies on an equally familiar phenomenon, the 'keystone' effect, when a projection screen is not square-on to the projector. Think of the enlarger as a projector, and the enlarger easel as the projection screen. By setting up the enlarger and easel properly, you can cancel out the 'falling-over-backwards' effect with the 'keystone' effect.

USING LONGER LENSES

You will get more even illumination for perspective correction if you use a longer-than-standard enlarger lens. When you correct verticals in the way described, one side of the image is clearly closer to the light source than the other. With a 50mm 'standard' enlarging lens on 35mm, or a 40mm wide-angle lens, this can result in unacceptable variations in exposure. A longer lens, such as an 80mm designed for roll-film negatives, will require a greater head elevation on the column but should improve the evenness of illumination.

▲ *Converging verticals*

The building sides converge because the camera was tilted upwards during the exposure. A perspective-control (PC) or shift lens can solve the problem, but these are not available for all models.

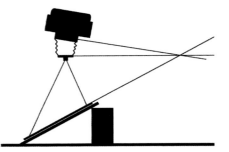

◄ *The Scheimpflug condition*

This is easier to set up by eye than it is to measure. When all three planes – negative, lens panel and enlarging easel – coincide at a single line, this is the Scheimpflug condition and everything will be in focus: there is no need to stop down.

CORRECTING PERSPECTIVE IN THE CAMERA

The easiest way to avoid the 'falling-over-backwards' effect is by using a shift lens (or a camera with a rising front) when you take the picture – unfortunately, shift lenses are very expensive. They work by moving the lens parallel with the film plane, as illustrated. As long as the film plane and the subject remain parallel, there will be no 'falling over backwards'.

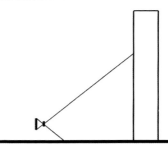

Normal position

With the lens in its normal position, it is impossible to get the whole of the building in without tilting the camera.

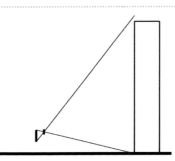

Raised lens

By raising the lens, but leaving the film where it is, the image moves upwards on the film and it is possible to get the whole building in.

◀ *Advanced
perspective control*
*A more sophisticated
form of perspective
control, shown here in
close-up, makes use of
a tilting negative stage
and/or lens panel, not
found on all enlargers.
This allows the
Scheimpflug condition
(opposite) to be
achieved, so you do not
need to stop down.*

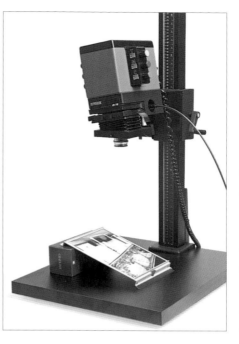

◀ *Simple perspective
control*
*The simplest form of
control involves propping
up one edge of the
enlarging easel with
books, so that the
'keystone' effect cancels
out the 'falling-over-
backwards' effect. If you
do not have a tilting
lens stage, you have to
stop the enlarger lens
down well, in order to
get adequate depth of
field, resulting in
long exposures.*

◀ *'Keystone' effect*
*The 'keystone' effect,
even with the
Scheimpflug condition
satisfied, means that
the image is keystone-
shaped, so quite heavy
cropping is essential.*

▶ *Parallel verticals*
*The corrected version
of the original picture
no longer exhibits the
'falling-over-backwards'
effect, but a certain
amount has been lost
from the edges.*

COMPUTER CORRECTION

Another way to correct the 'falling-over-backwards' effect is to scan in
the original print (or even the negative); manipulate it in Photoshop or
a similar program; and then print it out. This has the advantage that you
can also 'stretch' the image vertically in order to emphasize the sense
of height. Plan lines are easy, too. But somehow, it just isn't the same.

AFTERWORK

In this chapter, we look at the techniques that can (and often must) be applied after the print has been processed. As so often in darkroom work, these techniques are not particularly difficult. It is, however, even more difficult to 'save' an indifferent print through technically skilled afterwork than it is to 'save' an indifferent negative through technically skilled printing. Each stage builds on the previous one: good negative, good print, good afterwork, good presentation – the technical quality of a print is only as good as the technical quality of the least excellent step in the sequence.

The most fundamental difference is that a bad photographer will look at a work print and say, 'Good enough', where a good one will crop, dodge and burn to get a better print. Next, the good photographer will carefully spot out dust marks. These two steps alone mark a massive change in attitude.

SPOTTING

Dust is a besetting problem for photographers, especially 35mm photographers, whose pictures are so greatly enlarged that even the tiniest mote starts to look like a beam. Obviously, every attempt must be made at every stage to avoid dust, but with the best will in the world, it affects everyone sooner or later.

The old name for print spotting is 'print finishing', and hoary-bearded ancients are fond of pointing out that a print is not really finished until it has been spotted. They are right. The difference between an unspotted print and one that has been finished is extraordinary. The choice is between working with dyes, pigments and SpotPens.

◀ Dyes

Dyes sink into the emulsion and become invisible, but if you get your retouching wrong they are difficult or impossible to remove. They are diluted to give the precise shade of grey needed, and are often made in 'standard' and 'warm' tones, although in any retouching, if you match the tone, the colour is unlikely to show. They are available from a number of manufacturers.

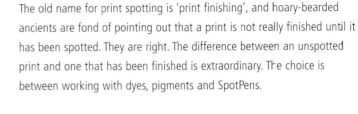

◀ SpotPens

SpotPens are dyes in a slightly viscous medium. They can easily be wiped off for a few seconds after they are applied, but they eventually sink into the emulsion and become invisible. Because they cannot easily be mixed or diluted, they are sold in packs of 10 graded greys, in both 'warm' and 'standard' tones. Unlike conventional dyes or pigments, they do not darken as they dry.

▲ Pigments

Pigments are easy to remove, but stand on the surface, leaving a patch that is a different texture to the rest of the print. Like dyes, they are diluted to match specific greys: they can even be mixed with other colours to match specific image tones. Specialist pigments – even 'paint boxes' like this one from Kaiser – are available from a number of manufacturers, or you can just use any good-quality pigment.

useful tips

• SpotPens should be tested with each new paper, as they work much better with some than with others. With Ilford Multigrade IV we always use SpotPens; with Multigrade Warmtone we use dyes instead.

• You can use a white tile or plate as a palette for dyes or pigments.

• It is much more important to match tone than to match colour. A plain grey dye or pigment will normally disappear against even a very warm-toned or cool-toned print.

• To match spotting pigments to the image colour, add burnt sienna or burnt umber to plain black for warmer tones, or deep blue to the black for cooler tones.

• To match dyes to the image colour, especially in toned prints, use colour retouching dyes.

using spotting media

If you have difficulty in focusing very close, try a pair of very-close-focusing spectacles (to prescription, or even from the supermarket), or try to find a watchmaker's head band. You will also find it easier to work under a good, strong light such as an Anglepoise. If you are using dye or pigment, work with an almost-dry brush, diluting the tone on the palette before trying it on a scrap print. With a SpotPen, the tone on the body of the pen is an extraordinarily accurate guide to the colour of the spot. Because the dye sits on the surface for a while, you need to wait for it to soak in.

▶ *1 This print of Mnajdra, in Malta, has the most appalling hair over it – deliberately draped across the negative, we hasten to add, to show how much can be retouched out.*

◀ *2 Protect the print that you are working on with a sheet of paper, to stop your hand sticking to it. You will also need a palette if you are using dyes or pigments. Use the border of a scrap print (on the same sort of paper) to judge the depth of tone that is needed. Break up large areas with a series of dabs or ticks; do not attempt to 'paint in' a hair or large spot.*

▶ *3 Join up the dabs or ticks with other ticks. With a little practice, the hair can be made invisible.*

black spots

The easiest way to deal with black spots is to bleach them back to white and then spot in the area as described above. The traditional approach was to 'knife' the black spot, scraping away the emulsion with a very sharp scalpel, but this is even more difficult with modern emulsions than it was in the past, and rarely works at all with RC papers.

1 Keep one brush exclusively for bleach/reducer, to avoid contamination – mark it with a dab of paint on the handle. For mixing and using the bleach, follow the instructions that come with it; some are best used on a damp (not wet) print. A convenient bleach is strong Farmer's Reducer (see page 90).

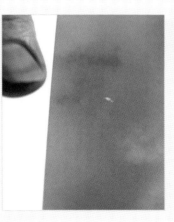

2 When the spot is bleached away, rewash the print as if it had just come from the fixing bath. Otherwise, the bleached spot may later stain.

3 When the print is fully washed, dry and spot conventionally, using either SpotPens or (as here) dye on a brush.

LOCAL BLEACHING

The use of bleach to remove black spots has already been covered on page 89, but here we are concerned with using weaker bleach to lighten selected areas and add impact. The normal bleach is Farmer's Reducer, made up from 'hypo' and 'pot ferri' or potassium ferricyanide. (Despite its name, pot ferri is nothing like as dangerous as cyanide.)

Clouds, the whites of the eyes in a portrait, chromium on a car – there is no end to what you can lighten with Farmer's Reducer. Before trying it on a good, final print, however, experiment with a few scrap prints, both for the sake of your own technique and to make sure that the paper responds well: with some papers, there can be an unacceptable colour shift, especially if bleaching is carried too far.

Farmer's Reducer is normally sold in small sachets which are mixed up to give two long-lived stock solutions, or they can be made from the raw chemicals. One is approximately 12.5 per cent hypo, and the other is approximately 10 per cent pot ferri: the exact concentration is not critical. For use, take 100 ml (3.8 fl oz) of hypo solution and add 5 ml (0.16 fl oz) of the pot ferri solution. You can add more pot ferri for a faster action, up to 12 ml (0.38 fl oz), but it may be inconveniently rapid. The working solution is lemon-yellow, and remains active for only a few minutes: a blue-green tinge indicates that it has gone off.

Before mixing the Farmer's Reducer, soak the print and wipe or pat it dry; you want to work on a print that is damp, but not flooded. As noted on page 88, keep one brush exclusively for reducer, to avoid contamination: mark it with a dab of paint on the handle. As with spotting brushes, the higher the quality of the brush, the easier it will be to use.

◄ *Catching the moment*

Very carefully, working on a damp print, paint on the Farmer's Reducer. Just before the area to be lightened has reached the right density, flood it with water and wash until the yellow tinge is no longer visible: the reducer continues to work as it is being washed out. You can always repeat the reducing process if you need to, but you cannot easily add density that has been removed. Repeat, lightening other areas as needed. When you have finished, wash the print as if it had just come from the fixing bath (which, in effect, it has). Use wash aid on fibre-based prints to save time. Dry normally.

◄ *Making choices*

Despite the caveat for the picture opposite, do not let your knowledge of how the view really looked stop you reworking it closer to how you wanted it to look.

useful tips

• If the Farmer's Reducer works too fast, dilute it to half strength or even quarter strength.

• Some papers change colour more than others when locally bleached, so if you use more than one kind of paper, test the bleach for each type.

• Practise on scrap prints before applying this technique to important pictures.

• Consider making two or three identical prints so that you can compare the effects of different degrees of bleaching.

▲ *Dramatic lightening*

The strong, dramatic shape of this cordage demanded fairly high contrast; but then, the frayed ends went too dark. The answer? Farmer's Reducer, also known as 'liquid sunshine'.

▶ *Increased differences*

Here, we have increased the differentiation at the edges of the clouds, to give a much more dramatic effect. Be careful not to over-bleach, because any effect that announces its presence too clearly is a failure.

SEPIA TONING

Sepia-toning is used for various reasons: for an 'olde-worlde' look, for increased archival permanence, or simply because it looks good. Some people use toning as a way to improve indifferent pictures, sometimes successfully: in particular, flat, soft pictures often look a lot better toned than they do untoned. Practise on old work prints and unsuccessful pictures to get a feel for how far you need to bleach, and what effects you can get.

Today, almost all sepia-toning is done by a two-bath process. The print is first bleached, then the image is brought back in an odourless thiourea-based bath. The older sodium-sulphide version uses the same bleach, but a different second bath. It gives a warmer tone, less yellow and tending more towards peach or red, but unfortunately the sulphide bath gives off an overpowering (and poisonous) smell of rotten eggs. Some maintain that the best results of all are obtainable with the even older single-bath, hypo-alum hot-toning process, which stinks so badly that it is normally done out of doors.

As so often in darkroom work, the only real way to see if a particular paper and sepia toner will work together is to try them. Some give pleasing tones in combination; others don't. A lot depends, in addition, on the print developer; on how hard or soft the water is in your area; and, as usual, on that liberal dose of alchemy that tempers the hard science of photography.

 ## the sepia-toning process

In general, the ideal print for sepia-toning looks very much like any other print. It does not normally need to be printed lighter or darker. It is, however, worth saying that soft, flat prints are more often improved by toning than contrasty ones. You will learn a lot from practising on work prints and even on test strips (provided they are fully fixed and washed), just to see what happens.

1 Any conventional print, on RC or FB paper, can be toned: this is Stone's River (Murfreesboro), a famous battlefield of the American Civil War. If the print is dry, soak it in plain water for a few minutes before transferring to the bleach bath.

2 Agitate constantly during bleaching, which may be stopped at any stage. After 15 seconds, only the highlights have begun to disappear. To slow bleaching, dilute the bleach further.

3 As bleaching progresses, the image gets 'warmer' and only the darker tones are clearly visible. If you stopped bleaching at this stage, the result would be something like in step six below.

4 Eventually, after several minutes, only a faint, yellowish image remains. After bleaching, whether full or partial, the print is washed until the yellow stain from the bleach disappears from the borders of the print. This should take about two minutes for RC paper and five to ten minutes for FB.

5 The bleached, washed print is then placed in the toner until it has fully toned. This typically takes anything from a few seconds to five minutes, depending on the toner in use. The toned print is then washed in running water for five minutes (RC) or 30 minutes (FB) and dried normally.

6 **Partial bleaching**
Partial bleaching makes for a richer, browner print, though a great deal depends on the precise formula of the bleach (see box on right) and the toner.

7 **Full bleaching**
Full bleaching makes for a yellower print. This often looks more Victorian, especially when combined with a slightly under-exposed, low-contrast print.

LIFE, CAPACITIES AND ADDITIVES

Both bleaches and toners can normally be reused until their action becomes unacceptably slow, though working solutions will deteriorate (that is, become slower and slower in action) whether they are used or not. Concentrates in part-full bottles last for three to six months; unopened concentrates should last for a year or more.

Most thiourea-based toners are supplied with an additive that can be mixed with the toner in varying proportions to change the colour from more yellow to more ginger. Once the additive is in the toner, of course, it cannot be taken out again – so experiment with small volumes!

OTHER TONERS

Although sepia is the most familiar form of toning, there are other colours that can be achieved: it is even possible to use two toners sequentially, giving one colour in the shadows and another in the highlights. The most usual colours are blue/green (iron) and red (usually copper), though others, including yellow (today titanium or vanadium, formerly cadmium) are available from some manufacturers.

Gold and selenium toners often have a comparatively small effect on image colour, but they can greatly prolong the life of the print by reducing the susceptibility of the silver image to attack from pollutants. Most other metal toners either have no influence on archival permanence, or actually make the prints more susceptible to atmospheric attack.

Some are 'indirect' toners, like sepia, where the image is first bleached and then redeveloped in the toner to give a coloured image, while others are 'direct': the print is first soaked in water for a minute or so (or taken direct from the wash), then immersed in the toner until the desired colour is achieved.

It is also possible to make 'chromogenic' toners, which use a bleach-and-redevelop system like an indirect toner: the dye image is formed at the same time as the silver is redeveloped, as it is in a colour film. The silver image may then be left in place, for added density, or bleached out to leave only the bright dye image. The usual approach is to make up four stock solutions of colour couplers, for magenta, yellow, cyan and blue, and to mix them in different proportions for different colours. The couplers (dye precursors) are complex organic chemicals: for example, p-nitrobenzyl cyanide for magenta. If you want to try this, you can find formulae in old photography journals and books.

Different papers react to different toners in different ways, and as with sepia toning, the only way to see how a particular toner works with a given paper is to try it, preferably on a scrap print to begin with. Warm-tone papers, in particular, may show dramatic colour shifts with selenium, where the same toner has very little effect on cold-tone papers. Also, the quality of the water supply can have some effect, especially on blue toners.

◀ *Blue*

Most blue (iron) toners are direct. They are particularly sensitive to water quality: patchy colour shifts and uneven toning indicate that it would be a good idea to use purified water. Most iron toners intensify the image and increase contrast slightly, so prints for toning should be made slightly lighter (maybe a quarter-stop less exposure) and slightly less contrasty (maybe a quarter-grade) than normal. Fully toned using Paterson blue toner on Ilford Multigrade Warmtone.

▲ *Red*

Red (copper) toners are direct, and have little or no effect on the depth or density of the print. Partial toning gives a purplish-black. Fully toned using Paterson red toner on Ilford Multigrade IV.

◄ Red and blue

Sequentially toning in first red (for the highlights) and then blue (for the shadows) gives an unusual effect, with crossover in the mid-tones leading to a red-blue. The more contrasty parts of the image, such as the boat, better illustrate the highlight/shadow divide. Paterson red and blue on Ilford Multigrade Warmtone.

◄ Selenium

Selenium direct toning gives a purplish tone if well extended; in the shorter term, it gives a slightly plum or aubergine hue to the blacks. The same toner has a much less marked effect on plain Multigrade IV. Paterson selenium on Ilford Multigrade Warmtone.

▲ Sepia and gold

Toning with first sepia (an indirect toner), then with gold (direct) gives colours that are variously described as 'peachy', 'pink' and 'orange'. Paterson toners on Ilford Multigrade IV.

◄ Bleach, sepia and gold

The effect of any toner can be greatly modified by reducing the time for which it acts. This print was partially bleached before being sepia toned and then finished in gold toner. The darker areas look almost green, but this is by comparison with the orange of the lighter areas. Paterson toners on Ilford Multigrade Warmtone.

HAND-COLOURING — OILS

Hand-colouring has two great attractions. One is that it allows you to do things which are not possible with conventional colour photography. The other, which is somewhat less expected, is that it is remarkably easy to learn. You can be as subtle, or as vivid, as you like – and, of course, you do not have to restrict yourself to the original, true colours. Indeed, if you do want to remain faithful to the original, you may need a colour reference print to remind you.

You can use almost any media for hand-colouring, from felt-tip pens to food dyes to a child's paint box, but those that are specifically made for hand colouring are often easier to use and are likely to prove more archivally permanent. There are three main groups of choices: oils, dyes and SpotPens, though coloured pencils can also be used. The most suitable prints are often a little lighter than usual, and sepia toning is surprisingly often a good preliminary.

Each hand-colouring medium requires slightly different techniques for application, so we have covered oils on this page and dyes and SpotPens on pages 98–99. The only thing that needs to be said about coloured pencils is that you need a fairly light touch, or you get ugly shiny patches, and that slightly matt surfaces are needed to provide a 'tooth' to take the colour. All other media can be used on both glossy and matt prints.

useful tips

- Don't overwork the print. Subtle colouring is often more effective than heavy afterwork.

- Several light applications can often be more effective than one heavy one.

application techniques

Oils may be applied as a transparent medium, so that you can clearly see the picture through them, or as an opaque medium, obscuring the photograph beneath. Perhaps the biggest surprise is that for transparent colouring (the usual approach), you do not use a brush very much. Rather, the colour is applied with cotton buds; with cotton wool in a pad; or with cotton wool on the tip of a wooden skewer.

Use either a disposable palette, where you tear off the top sheet, and start with a new palette for each session, or (as here) disposable plates. If you do use disposable plates, you can cover them with cling film, freeze them, then use them again at a later session.

▶ *1 A plastic plate makes a good disposable palette, and cotton buds make good disposable brushes. Buy tubs of cheap cotton buds: there is no need for expensive sterile buds. These are Marshall's Transparent Photo Oils, but you can also buy photo oils from Veronica Cass. Blend colours in small quantities: use neutral Extender to reduce saturation.*

◀ *2 With a circular, 'scribbling' motion and a very light touch, apply the colour and blend it into the picture. Do not worry if the cheeks look like a toy soldier's at first: a little gentle spreading with the cotton bud will soon even the colour out.*

◀ *3 For finer work than is possible with a cotton bud, wrap a little cotton wool around the tip of a bamboo skewer or wooden toothpick. The slightest dab of glue on the skewer, before you attach the cotton wool, may help the cotton to stay in place.*

◄ *4* Cotton wool on a skewer is useful for areas such as the lips and eyes, but once again, it is worth repeating that you need a light touch.

◄ *5* Pick up excess colour, or blend colours, or spread the colour, with fresh cotton buds or cotton-on-a-skewer, replacing them when necessary. They are not expensive!

◄ *6* A clean bud can lift almost all the colour, and any more can be removed with Marlene (the Marshalls solvent) on another clean bud or cotton-on-a-skewer. This is ideal for cleaning up areas like the whites of the eyes. It is surprising how casual, even Fauve, you can be with the colouring, and clean it up later.

◄ *7* For larger areas of colour, apply generously in big loops with a cotton bud to get the maximum coverage as quickly as possible.

▲ *8* Blend uneven colour with cotton-wool balls. Do not worry about 'bleeding' into the borders: you can clean these up later, or conceal them when you mount the print (see pages 100–103).

▲ *Flesh tones coloured*
Very different effects can be achieved by trying out colour alternatives. In this portrait of Sophie, only the flesh tones have been coloured.

▲ *Flesh tones uncoloured*
A complete reversal of the areas coloured presents an equally attractive result. In this picture, only the flesh tones have been left uncoloured.

HAND-COLOURING —
DYES AND SPOTPENS

Because the colours from both dyes and SpotPens sink into the emulsion, the surface texture of the print is unaffected. In extreme cases, it is possible to fool people into thinking that they are seeing a conventional colour photograph — except that they can see that the colours aren't right. It is always rather good for the ego when they ask, 'How did you do that?' Practise on scrap paper first to learn how to apply colours evenly, especially intense colours.

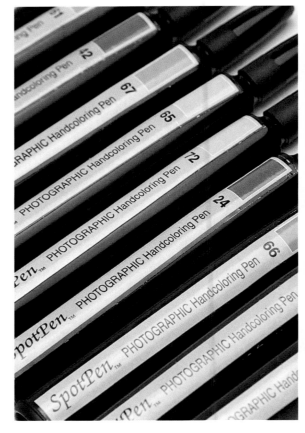

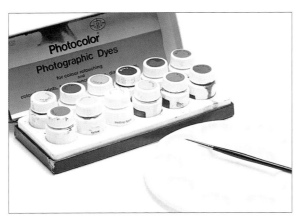

◄ *Dyes*

Most dyes, like these from Paterson, come in small plastic bottles and are very intense. They are diluted with water, preferably with a couple of drops of wetting solution in it (see page 14), and mixed on an impervious palette: traditionally ceramic, nowadays often plastic.

▲ *SpotPens*

SpotPens consist of photographic dyes ready loaded into felt-tip pens. They are significantly more expensive: a single set of 10 costs as much as a full set of dyes, and you really need two or three sets.

▲ *Peerless dyes*

Peerless dyes are unusual in that they are impregnated into what looks like blotting paper. Either a tiny bit of paper is torn off and dropped in the water, or a corner of the paper is simply dipped in the water (but watch out for cross-contamination of wet sheets if you do this). Again, adding a drop or two of wetting solution to the water will make it easier to apply, and it will sink in faster without 'beading'.

useful tip

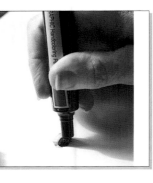

Before you use a SpotPen hand-colouring pen for the first time, it is a good idea to soften the tip by 'squishing' it against a hard surface such as a tile or saucer. Dipping it in clean water first may make this easier.

using spotpens

Because they are the easiest dye medium to use, we have concentrated on SpotPens here. If you use dyes and brushes, you can still blend colours on the print but it is somewhat easier to get unwanted streaks and blotches because the dyes sink in faster. Soaking and rubbing will remove some dye, but not all.

useful tip

USING FILTERS

Regardless of which hand-colouring medium you choose, remember that you can use filters at the taking stage to make it easier to hand-colour the pictures. For instance, if you photograph a red rose without a filter, it may come out rather dark. Use a red filter to lighten it.

1 Dampen the surface of the print with a little distilled water plus wetting solution. Some tap waters may affect colours: very chalky water can give browns a violet tint, for example.

2 If you can use Magic Markers, or a child's colouring set, you can use SpotPens. The colours are applied and blended on the surface of the print.

3 The dye from SpotPens can be lightened or further blended with the help of a damp sponge on the print.

4 SpotPen colour-retouching pens were designed for spotting colour prints, but are also ideal for hand-colouring small areas. Alternatively, use other media such as conventional dyes (on a very fine brush) or even coloured pencils. There is nothing wrong with mixing your media.

5 This picture took well under 30 minutes to colour, including time out to shoot the step-by-step pictures. With minimal practice, you should be able to achieve similar effects in 15 or 20 minutes.

ADHESIVE-MOUNTING AND DRY-MOUNTING

It is only natural to want to display a picture that you are proud of, and although the skills of mounting and display are not exclusively photographic, you can greatly enhance the appearance of your pictures by taking a little care in this area.

For just an occasional picture, especially if it is given as a gift, commercial framing services can be entirely appropriate, and surprisingly affordable. For pictures to be displayed for a few months, weeks or even days, there is no need to worry much about archival permanence, but if you want the picture to last for as long as possible, it is a good idea to use 'archival' materials and techniques.

Old-fashioned adhesives are not recommended: rubber solution and many other adhesives are rich in sulphur, which can attack untoned prints, and starch paste invites insect attack. Also, it is hard to avoid lumps when using most glues. Modern spray adhesives, specially designed for photographic mounting, are better. Alternatively, you can buy sticky-backed foam-core board: it is expensive, and you have to be careful not to stick the print down wrong, but it is very convenient. Start at one side, and work across, to avoid air bubbles.

Dry-mounting is best of all. It generally gives better adhesion at the corners, and even with non-archival board, dry-mounting tissue helps isolate the print from contaminants in the board. The 20 x 25-cm (8 x 10-in) dry-mounting press in the pictures was probably made in the 1950s. It is less convenient than a bigger, more modern press, but presses like this can sometimes be found very cheaply at camera fairs or the like. It is possible to dry mount small prints using a domestic iron, but this is not easy.

HANGING PICTURES

A traditional way to hang plain, mounted prints is with stick-on tabs: one end sticks to the mount, and the other has an eyelet in it. You can use a single tab, and hang the picture from the eyelet, or twin tabs, and tie a piece of string between the eyelets.

Another approach is to use sticky-backed Velcro or similar hook-and-loop material. Put one piece on the wall — it may, of course, mark paint or wallpaper when it is removed — and the corresponding piece on the back of the print. Many pictures at photo shows are 'hung' like this. You can even 'hang' reasonably light glazed frames in this way if you use enough Velcro, though some public spaces forbid the use of glass as a safety hazard.

useful tips

HEAT CONTROL
• Most dry-mounting presses have some form of heat control, which is very useful. If the tissue sticks to the print but not the mount, the press probably is not hot enough; if it sticks to the mount but not the print, the press is probably too hot, or pressure was applied for too long.

• Pre-warming the mount (before you tack on the print) is often a good idea.

dry-mounting

For maximum archival permanence, use archival board such as Arquati, as cheap boards may contain acids that will attack the image. Good camera stores may stock dry-mounting tissue and archival boards: otherwise, go to a picture-framers' supplier (look in the Yellow Pages).

1 Cut a piece of dry-mounting tissue slightly larger than the print, and tack it down in the middle. You can buy purpose-made tacking irons, or use a domestic iron, or even a small soldering iron. Do not press too hard or you will mark the front of the print.

2 Trim the tissue to the size of the print. You can use a razor blade or scalpel and straightedge, but a purpose-made cutter like this Rotatrim is much easier.

3 Tack the corners of the dry-mounting tissue to the mounting board. Be careful to avoid wrinkles, and beware of grit or dust, which will be revealed mercilessly when the print is mounted.

4 Place a sheet of silicone release paper on top of the print-tissue-board sandwich. This removes the risk of the print or mount sticking to the dry-mounting press. The silicone release paper can be reused repeatedly.

5 Compress the whole sandwich in the dry-mounting press for about 30 seconds. Some presses take as little as 10–15 seconds; others may benefit from as much as 60 seconds.

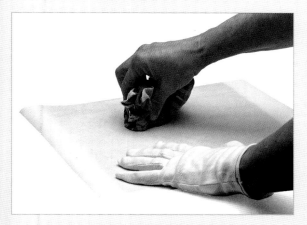

6 A useful trick is to remove the mounted print from the press, place it on a hard, smooth surface, and, with the silicone release paper still in place, rub down the print from one corner to the other using a soft cloth, forcing everything into contact and driving out air bubbles.

7 Flex the mounted print to make sure that it is firmly stuck down. If it is not, you can always run it through the dry-mounting press again.

WINDOW MOUNTS
AND FRAMES

More and more photographers are adopting an almost Victorian approach to pictures on their walls: the more, the better. Many mix their own pictures with pictures by friends, or even with pictures they have bought. Quite apart from the pleasure of exchanging pictures, there is always the cheering thought that if one of you becomes famous, the others will have something valuable on the wall!

There are three approaches to buying actual frames. One is to go to a commercial framer, and have your frames made to order. The second is to buy cheap, ready-made frames, and put your pictures in mounts to suit the sizes available. Given how cheap ready-made frames can be, this is an option well worth considering. The third is to learn how to make frames, and to buy a stock of frame-making materials, so that you can make frames of uniform appearance in a range of sizes. This is probably only worthwhile if you want to sell your pictures in frames, and want to establish a particular uniform style.

With either of the latter two approaches, it is extremely useful if you can cut your own window mounts, rather than having to rely on flush-mounting. Normally, window mounts look better than flush mounts, and they also have the advantage that they act as a spacer, so that the photograph is not pressed hard against the glass, where it may stick or even begin to deteriorate.

Using a commercial bevel cutter is so much easier than trying to use a scalpel and straightedge that we make no apology for considering only

the former approach. With the scalpel and straightedge, even if you can cut straight, holding the bevel angle constant and accurate is extremely difficult and tiring.

MOUNT SIZES AND COLOURS

The size and colour of mount that a particular print needs is as subjective (and often as unexpected) as the size that a print 'wants' to be. There is no doubt, however, that the right size (and colour) mount can greatly enhance a print, and it is worth keeping a selection of mount sizes and colours so that you can see what will suit a particular image. Too big a mount can look pretentious; too small a mount can look insignificant. And, of course, the colour of the mount can be as much a question of matching the mount to the decor of the place where it will be hung, as of matching it to the print.

PLACING THE PRINT

The best way to check how prints will look in a mount is to have a selection of mounts in different sizes and colours, and simply to place the print on the mounts. Alternatively, you can do it electronically: scan in both the mount and the print, and superimpose them in Adobe Photoshop or a similar program. Of course, the colours won't be the same, but you do have the enormous advantage that you can vary the sizes of the print and the mount independently.

◀ *Off-centre placing*
Often, a print looks best if it is not absolutely central in the mount. At least, the lower border normally looks better if it is wider than the upper border.

◀ *Landscape and portrait*
Sometimes, you can even put a landscape (horizontal) print into a portrait (vertical) mount; the other way around is less often successful.

◀ *Asymmetrical mounting*

Asymmetric mounts like this go in and out of style, but with the right subject they can work well. There is also plenty of room to sign the mount, though this is a matter for your own conscience.

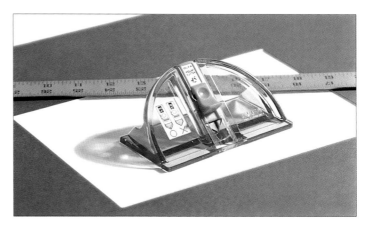

▲ *Bevel-edged cutter*

Bevel-edged cutters like this Olfa are comparatively inexpensive and need only a straightedge for guidance. Olfa also makes an oval mount cutter, which can be particularly effective with portraits, especially vignetted ones – but it is considerably trickier to use than the straight-line cutter.

using a bevel-edged cutter

The blades in the Olfa cutter used here are interchangeable and double-ended, so that they can be reversed when one end is blunt: sharp blades make mount-cutting much easier.

1 The secret of successful cutting with the Olfa (and other cutters like it) is to make each cut several times, running a little deeper each time, rather than trying to slice through the whole board at once. Use a sheet of cardboard under the mount, to avoid blunting the blade too rapidly.

2 Cut from the back, where you have marked up the dimensions of the window. Rotate the mount, and always cut from the same direction (here, with the centre of the mount to the left of the cutting blade) to ensure that the bevel is always in the right direction. A bevel that slopes in the wrong direction is most vexing.

3 You can stick the photograph behind the window with self-adhesive tape, but ideally, you should dry-mount it first. It will be stronger and flatter if you do.

4 The bevelled edge gives a distinctive (and expensive) look to the print.

GOING FURTHER

In the house of photography, there are many mansions. Some people try to cover as broad a range as possible, while others become more and more fascinated with one aspect of the subject until they become a world-class expert. There are many areas in photography where an enthusiast, without formal education in the subject, can hold his or her own with the manufacturers' own representatives, and even teach them a thing or two – though it has to be said that when the opinions of the enthusiastic amateur and the manufacturer's expert diverge, it is generally safer to believe the expert.

There are countless paths and tangents that may turn out to be no more than an interesting (or frustrating!) afternoon's work, or may equally develop into a life-long interest. Just a few of them are suggested in this chapter.

BIGGER PRINTS

Somewhat unexpectedly, making really big prints is one of the most difficult and expensive things in this book. The materials are expensive; you need a lot of space; and the physical effort involved can be unreasonably tiring.

It therefore makes sense to look at three size levels. The first is larger than you can process in a reasonable-sized dish, up to say 30 x 40 cm (12 x 16 in). The second is the biggest you can process in any readily available dish, up to about 50 x 60 cm (20 x 24 in). And the third is bigger still.

ENLARGERS

Most enlargers allow a maximum size of around 30 x 40 cm (12 x 16 in), or sometimes 40 x 50 cm (16 x 20 in), on the baseboard. Some enlargers allow one of the approaches described below, but not the other; some allow both; and some allow neither.

PAPER

The largest cut size that is normally available is 40 x 50 cm (16 x 20 in), though 50 x 60 cm (20 x 24 in) is sometimes available. For still bigger prints, you can buy paper in rolls, typically up to 132 cm (52 in) wide.

The cheapest approach is probably to do a rough cut with a pair of scissors, and clean up the edges after processing. Resin-coated paper is much quicker and easier to wash than fibre-based.

PROCESSING PRINTS

Processing very large prints is likely to be a question of what you can fit into your darkroom and what you can afford, rather than what is objectively best.

Labs that specialize in giant prints normally use either processing machines, or huge, custom-made trays that hold vast volumes of developer and fixer.

▼ *Enlarging downwards*

Rotate the head on the column and project it over the edge of the bench onto the floor.

▼ *Troughs*

To process prints up to about 30 x 40 cm (12 x 16 in) in a small volume of developer, and without taking up too much counter space, build processing troughs from plastic guttering: seal the end joints with silicone rubber if need be. The trough should be at least 10 cm (4 in) longer than the maximum print width to be processed. Wear rubber gloves.

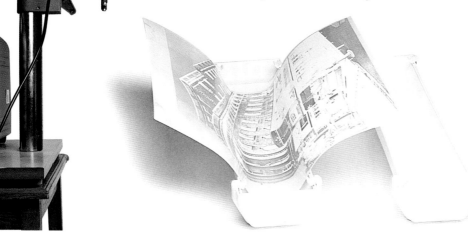

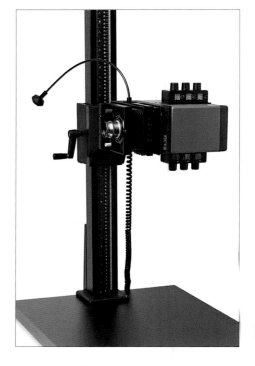

▲ *Enlarging side-on*

The other way of getting bigger enlargement sizes is to turn the enlarger head sideways on the column, so that you can project onto the wall. The remote drive cable makes it easier to get to the enlarged image while focusing.

◀ Large trays

Another technique is to build a single monster tray on the floor, using a wood frame and heavy polyethylene sheeting. Line the tray with newspaper; swab on the developer with a soft sponge; when the print is fully developed (five to ten minutes), mop up as much developer as you can, replace the newspaper, and swab on fixer with another sponge.

▲ *Trays*

The same technique used with the troughs can be used with trays. Here, Frances is processing a piece of paper 137 cm (54 in) long and 61 cm (24 in) wide in a 50 x 61-cm (20 x 24-in) tray. The trays need 5-6 l (1.3–1.6 gal) of chemistry, and developing for four or five minutes is normally essential to ensure even development. The trimmed size of the print will be about 50 x 122 cm (20 x 48 in).

◀ *Drying*

The only practical way to dry giant prints is normally to hang them on a line. Indoors, over the bath, is preferable, especially in the summer, when suicidal gnats seem attracted to the sticky gelatine, but RC paper dries fast enough that out of doors is often satisfactory.

▲ *Washing the print*

Depending on the size of your print, you may be able to wash it in the bath, or you may decide to hose it off in the garden, as here. Don't forget to rinse the back two or three times, as well as hosing the front for two to four minutes. Well-diluted fixer will not harm your garden: in fact, it is a good fertilizer.

EXPOSURE TIMES

Inevitably, exposure times are likely to be very long. The increase is proportional to the square of the distance in magnification, but with very long exposures (60 seconds or more) you may need to give a stop or two more exposure to allow for reciprocity failure, depending on the paper. The table below shows the increases for different sizes, based on a 7 x 'all-in' enlargement from 35mm onto 20 x 25-cm (8 x 10-in) paper, taking 10 seconds at a given aperture.

20 x 25 cm ...... (8 x 10 in) .... (7 x) .... 1.0 x .... 10 sec
30 x 40 cm ...... (12 x 16 in) .... (11 x; $(^{11}\!/_7)^2$) ..... 2.5 x .... 25 sec
40 x 50 cm ...... (16 x 20 in) .... (15 x; $(^{15}\!/_7)^2$) ..... 4.6 x .... 46 sec
50 x 75 cm ...... (20 x 30 in) .... (19 x; $(^{19}\!/_7)^2$) ..... 7.4 x .... 75 sec
75 x 115 cm ...... (30 x 45 in) .... (29 x; $(^{29}\!/_7)^2$) ..... 17.0 x .... 180+ sec or more

If normal exposure for an 20 x 25-cm (8 x 10-in) print is 15 seconds, a 40 x 50-cm (16 x 20-in) print will be 60 seconds and a 100 x 150-cm (40 x 60-in) print will be 7 $\frac{1}{2}$ minutes.

SPECIAL EMULSION SUPPORTS

Most people use resin-coated glossy paper most of the time. Some prefer the tactile qualities of fibre-based paper, and untoned FB may last longer on display (for toned prints, or in dark storage, there is little or nothing in it). But there are numerous specialist papers; there are coated linens and coated metal sheets; and for the ultimate in flexibility, you can coat almost anything with liquid emulsions.

Most specialist papers are chosen for their textures and tactile qualities – and many are graded, not variable-contrast, so you need a negative that will print well on grade 2. Probably the widest range of textures is offered by Kentmere (sold as Luminos in the USA); probably the most luxurious paper is a special, heavyweight watercolour paper that is specially coated for Bergger in France. Bergger also supplies thin, light alloy sheets coated with photographic emulsion. These were originally intended for making one-off or limited-production instruction plates and other labels for machinery.

In addition, several manufacturers sell photo linen, which (after printing) can be cut, sewn and even washed, leading to the potential for remarkable, if somewhat stiff, garments. The emulsion is grade 2 only, and the fabric goes rather floppy during processing, but these are the only drawbacks to photo linen.

LIQUID EMULSIONS

Several makes of liquid emulsion are available, and with them, you can coat virtually anything: stones, china, old toys, crash helmets... Unlike photo linen, the coating is not very durable, and will soon wash off if used out of doors, though varnishing a fully dry image can solve this problem.

Most liquid emulsions are single grade (typically grade 2), though a few – notably Maco – are variable-contrast. The variable contrast is, however, of disputable value, as variations in coating thickness are likely to mask much of the variable-contrast effect.

Only a few 'sized' papers and (unexpectedly) emulsion paints are suitable for the direct application of liquid emulsions. Unsized papers, and all other surfaces, are best 'subbed' with plain gelatine solution. The Maco liquid-emulsion 'system' includes gelatine for this purpose. You can use diluted liquid emulsion, but it must be dried in the dark or it will 'print out' and go muddy-grey.

useful tips

• Hand-coated paper will keep for several days at least, and can be exposed, processed and washed much like any other photographic paper.

• If you decide that rough edges and even blank areas are a part of your technique, you can be more casual about applying emulsion.

• For longer life and reduced fog, store emulsions in the fridge, but take them out for an hour or two before you need to use them.

 ## using liquid emulsion

To 'sub' the surface, make up a gelatine solution in warm water – about a teaspoon in a cup – and paint this on in the same way as the liquid emulsion (see illustration). This step can be done in normal lighting. It is important that you allow the gelatine to dry fully before applying the liquid-emulsion coat.

1 Working under the safelight, remove some liquid emulsion from the bottle with a plastic spoon and place in a suitable small container: we use a small stainless-steel film tank, which can be handled in room lighting once the lid is on. Warm the container in hot water at about 45° C (115°F); do not go much above 50°C (122°F) or you risk harming the emulsion.

HARDENING AND WASHING

One of the biggest difficulties is keeping the emulsion on the support during processing, especially washing. Adding a little hardener to the subbing coat or emulsion before coating, and allowing extra drying time, will help, as will adding hardener to the developer. The Maco Black Magic system consists of emulsion, subbing gelatine and hardener. Even so, it is as well to wash very gently (and keep wet time to a minimum, using a wash aid) to reduce the risk of the emulsion coming off. This is particularly true if you are working on hard, non-porous surfaces such as glazed tile or stones.

▶ *Printing on watercolour paper*

This long-abandoned powder magazine at the copper mines of Santas Domingos in Portugal was printed on a heavy, handmade watercolour paper that was first subbed with gelatine and then coated with Maco Black Magic liquid emulsion. Historical subjects often seem to suit hand-coated papers well.

▲ *Printing on coated stones*

These flints from a Kentish beach were well washed to remove salt; painted with white emulsion paint; then coated in much the same way as the paper (below). Two were printed with images of a Tibetan 'Mani' stone, with its painted prayers, and one was hand-coloured (see page 96). The third was printed with an image of Lenin's Tomb in Red Square, Moscow.

useful tip

• With some of the processes described in this book, it is essential to wear some sort of hand protection. Thin 'surgical' gloves can be bought cheaply in boxes of 100, and it is much safer and easier to use a new set of gloves fairly frequently than it is to rely on barrier creams, or (worse still) to dabble your unprotected skin in photographic solutions.

2 Almost any good hand-made paper will work for hand-coating. The easiest way to apply the emulsion is with a Japanese hake brush, which has no metal ferrule and so cannot contaminate the emulsion. Other brushes require more care. Paint top to bottom first...

3 ...then left to right, if you want even coating. Use a light touch; work in a warm room; and ideally, warm the paper while you are working on it – a Paterson dish warmer is ideal. Dry in a dark place. Hang from one corner or rest on a photo-quality blotter.

BROMOIL

Modern materials and processes are unbelievably good and unbelievably convenient. But there are plenty of other processes, stretching back almost to the dawn of photography, that have charms of their own. Some are pursued only by a few fanatics, while others are available as kits, or can be made up comparatively easily. There is only one, bromoil, that is suitable for enlarged prints.

Devotees of bromoil, which originated at the beginning of the 20th century, speak of its 'painterliness'; of how it is more than 'mere photography'; of its being a 'control process'. Its detractors call it 'muck-spreading'. In reproduction, even an excellent bromoil will often look all too like an inferior conventional print: you need to see an original in order to appreciate its beauty.

There is room only for a brief summary of the Bromoil process here: the easiest approach is to buy a kit, which supplies paper, chemicals, ink, an inking tile and a special bromoil brush known as a 'stag's foot'. This sequence was made using a Fotospeed kit. The only extra things you need are a palette knife (or old butter knife) and a sheet of heavy glass or plastic as a working surface. Inking a bromoil can easily take an entire afternoon. It is not unusual to experience a couple of failures before it comes right; the usual fault is over-inking.

making a bromoil print

Make the enlargement on special bromoil paper, or on any paper known to be suitable for bromoils: not all will work. Manufacturers of general-purpose papers rarely take much account of the needs of bromoilists, and may make unannounced changes which drastically affect the suitability of their papers for the process. The print should be of slightly lower-than-average contrast, but with as much detail as possible in the shadows. Fix and wash thoroughly.

Next, working with a tray in the usual fashion, put it in the bromoil bleach. Keep a tray specially for this, to avoid contaminating your usual trays. Agitate from time to time, until the image has all gone. As well as bleaching the image, the bleach hardens the emulsion in proportion to the intensity of the original image. If, for reasons of time, you have let the print dry before bleaching, soak it for 45 minutes or so in water at around 24°C (75°F) before it is bleached.

After bleaching, wash the print until the stain from the bleach disappears. Next, re-fix in a weak fixer, one part to nine instead of one part to three, and wash again for 20 minutes. The resulting 'matrix' looks like a sheet of blank paper. It can be inked up immediately, or left to dry. If it is left to dry, it will require soaking at 24°C (75°F), or a little more, for 20 minutes or so before inking. You can now start to apply the bromoil ink.

▶ *Folklore Museum, Gozo*

This enlargement of a corner of the museum has been printed with lower contrast than would be made under normal conditions; it is, however, right for bromoiling.

1 Stiff, greasy bromoil ink, needs to be kneaded or 'worked up' on a tile with a palette knife or old butter knife, to make it smooth to apply. The ink will adhere to the emulsion in direct proportion to how much the emulsion has been hardened.

2 Blot the wet matrix dry and lay it out on a stout, flat, waterproof working surface such as a heavy piece of glass or Perspex or Lucite. Inset: It is a good idea to make a second reference print, that is not bleached, to act as a guide when you are inking the bromoil.

3 Use a 'stag's foot' to apply the ink to the emulsion. Oil and water don't mix well, so the greasy ink sticks better to the more hardened areas of the emulsion. The motion used to apply the ink is often described as 'hopping'. Dabbing adds ink; dabbing-and-dragging removes ink. It is a good idea to start out with a contrasty area of the print, so you can see when things begin to happen.

4 Slowly the shapes start to emerge. If the matrix stops accepting ink, resoak it for a few minutes – it will look flat and horrible when you do this – then pat it dry again and keep bromoiling. You can add ink where you want more density (dabbing) and reduce ink where you want less (don't put it on to begin with, or dab-and-drag to remove it).

5 Put the bromoil somewhere warm, dry and dust-free for a few days until the ink is no longer tacky. A fully dried bromoil is as durable as any other photographic print, and because the image is made of pigment, not silver, it is more resistant to pollution than most.

LITH PRINTING

Lith – short for 'lithographic' – materials can be exploited to give unique effects. True lith images consist only of pure black and pure white with no greys, but this effect is much easier to achieve today via digital media. Modern lith depends on incomplete development, typically on incomplete infectious development, in weak, partially exhausted developer.

Infectious development means that the darker an area is, the faster it develops. The advantages of this are clear when you want only pure blacks and pure whites: dark areas soon go black, while light areas stay white. Using weak, partially exhausted developer slows down the development process greatly – and means that there is a longer 'window' between development starting, and going to finality.

This in turn means that if you 'snatch' the print before it is fully developed, only the darkest shadows will have turned black. Partial development of the mid-tones and highlights means that the silver image grains are very small, so these areas of the image will not be black. Instead, they will be yellow, brown, pink or even less likely colours.

PREPARING THE DEVELOPER
The first rule in lith is that exposure governs the dark areas, while development governs the light areas. The second is that to get the biggest possible window of opportunity, you need a large volume of developer, and ideally, you should 'prime' fresh developer with up to 25 per cent (by volume) of exhausted developer saved from a previous session.

useful tips

• Lith results are never fully repeatable because the developer is ageing all the time – but if you use a big enough volume of developer, you should be able to develop quite a few prints in the 'window' between fresh developer, which gives minimal lith effects, and complete developer exhaustion.

• If you do not have any used developer, fog a couple of sheets of paper by turning the room light on – old, inferior paper will do – and develop them to make sure you have some by-products in the developer.

Some lith developers work with non-lith papers, and some lith papers work in non-lith developers. Here, we used grade 2 Oriental G paper (not a specifically lith paper, though known to perform well in lith developer) and Maco lith developer, which works with a wide range of papers.

Dilute the developer to one quarter of the strength recommended in the manufacturer's instructions for true lith (pure black-and-white) use. Make up as much developer as you can fit into the largest tray you own. 4 l (108 fl oz) of developer in a 40 x 50 cm (16 x 20 in) tray is not too much for 20 x 25 cm (8 x 10 in) prints, though you can use normal-size trays for short stop and fixer.

EXPOSING THE PRINT
Start with four times the exposure you would give a non-lith print. Put the paper in the developer: it typically takes 15–30 minutes to develop a single print. Things happen very slowly at first, then faster and faster: after 20 minutes, you may have only a few seconds before development suddenly accelerates too fast and the print goes too dark. As soon as the shadow areas are black, immediately pull the paper out of the developer and put it in the short stop. After 30 seconds, fix normally.

◀ *Tattooed figure*
This lith print was made by Dr Tim Rudman,
probably the best-known (and arguably the best)
lith printer in the world. In addition to landscapes
and similar 'obvious' lith subjects, Dr Rudman
applies lith techniques to a very wide range of other
subjects, as much for the colour variations as for
the contrast effects for which lith is most noted.

▲ Typical lith effects

This lith print of the Houses of Parliament, Big Ben and other buildings exhibits the lith effect, with dramatic contrast and unusual image colours, but there is very little detail in the sky. This was exposed for 18 seconds and developed for about 15 minutes.

▲ Longer development

With the same exposure as before – 18 seconds – the print was developed for about 30 seconds longer. With lith development, you work by observation, not by time. There is still very little detail in the sky, but the buildings are beginning to 'block up' to a solid black.

▶ Longer exposure, shorter development

Quadrupling the exposure to 72 seconds, but 'snatching' the print even earlier than for the first picture, as soon as the first blacks began to appear, has given good differentiation in the buildings, plus tone in the sky – with characteristic lith colours.

EXPOSURE AND DEVELOPMENT

At first, it can be very confusing when you try to work out whether you need more or less exposure or more or less development. Fortunately, the rules are very simple.

If the dark areas are beginning to 'block up' before you get any highlight detail, you need more exposure and less development.

If development time is too short to allow you to 'snatch' the print during the 'window' between the darkening of the darkest areas and the mid-tones, you need less exposure and more development time.

HOME BREWS

In the early years of photography, everyone made everything from scratch – there are even recipes for making your own emulsions and coating your own plates in old books. As late as the 1950s and 1960s, many people still made up their own developers and other processing solutions from bulk chemicals.

Today, 'home brews' are unlikely to save you any money, and restrictions on the availability of bulk chemicals, some reasonable, others not, mean that mixing your own solutions from scratch is likely to be difficult as well as expensive. On the other hand, there are plenty of 'alternative' processes where you more or less have to mix up your own solutions, and some out-of-the-way developers are hard to buy off the shelf, so it may be more convenient to make them up from scratch.

Although home brewing is not difficult, you do need to understand which chemicals are dangerous and which are not – they should be clearly labelled – and you need to be reasonably careful, not mixing (or storing) chemicals in containers that are also used for food.

'ALTERNATIVE' PROCESSES

'Alternative' processes mostly date back to the 19th century, and are based on silver or on iron. Most produce brownish images on watercolour paper that has been printed with various chemicals to make it light-sensitive, though (for example) cyanotype produces blue images and platinotype gives very subtle pearly-greys. There are several modern books on alternative processes, or you can find out how they were done from old books. Provided you are careful with poisonous chemicals – and some of the chemicals used are very poisonous – these processes are rarely very difficult. Our Victorian ancestors were often quite casual about precise quantities, and still got excellent results.

SCALES AND CHEMICALS

For some purposes, such as making up hypo solutions, almost any scales or weighing machine will do: the Victorians, who invented modern photography, often used kitchen scales. Do not use the same scales for food and for photographic chemistry, however. For more accuracy, an Ohaus beam balance will allow you to weigh as little as 1 gm with an accuracy of around 20 per cent, or 5 gm to an accuracy of 5–10 per cent. For critical work, especially in compounding developers, you need a chemical balance (not shown) that will allow you to measure 0.5 gm to an accuracy of 0.01 gm (two per cent) – these are the sort of balances you may have used in the chemistry labs at school.

◀ *Volume and weight*

Many adherents of alternative processes work by volume, not by weight. The plastic cup illustrated holds near enough 100 gm of crystalline hypo: more than enough accuracy for making up a 20 per cent solution (500 ml of working solution), 10 per cent (1000 ml) or 5 per cent (2000 ml). The spoon holds 18 gm.

CHEMICALS AND SAFETY

Chemicals are generally best ordered from a specialist supplier to the photographic trade: suppliers advertise in the photographic press. Buying from general chemical dealers is often more expensive and may lead to problems if they decide that you are making bombs or drugs. Chemicals should be kept under lock and key if there is any danger of others gaining access to them. Formulae may be found in countless books, old and new, but be warned that some books contain copying and typographical errors which may render a given formula worthless. If in doubt, check two or more sources.

MAKING UP SOLUTIONS

• When making up solutions, pay careful attention to recommended temperatures. Too cold, and things can take forever to dissolve: too hot, and some chemicals may break down. Use about 66–75 per cent of the final volume to dissolve the chemicals, and make up to the final volume with cold water.

◄ *'Salt prints'*

'Salt prints' are made by impregnating a sheet of paper with common salt in a weak gelatine solution, then sensitizing it (in the dark) with silver nitrate solution. Contact prints can be made on this paper by 'printing out' (no development); toning (typically in a platinum toner); then fixing in weak hypo. All baths – salt, silver, toner and fixer – must be made up by the user. (Martin Reed, Silverprint)

► *'POP' paper*

'POP' (printing-out paper) is still manufactured by Kentmere and is available as Helios from Silverprint in London and from the Chicago Albumen Company in Housatonic, Massachusetts, USA. The paper is not developed: the contact-printed image 'prints out' during a long exposure to daylight or a strong UV source. It is toned in a home-brewed gold fixer, then fixed (after toning) in a weak hypo solution.

IMAGE MANIPULATION AND COMPUTERS

To a considerable extent, bromoil and lith – and even toning – are methods of non-digital image manipulation, but there are others, such as bleach-etch. There are also techniques that used to be done chemically, in a 'wet' darkroom, but which are so much easier to do electronically that they are almost never done any other way today. In fact, they are very seldom done at all, now that they are reasonably easy: the main reason for attempting them in the past was often curiosity, rather than a deep aesthetic need.

BLEACH ETCH

The images of the Dresden Opera House were all obtained by variations on the bleach-etch process. Several good kits are available: we have used both Tetenal and Fotospeed.

We have also tried to make up our own bleach-etch solutions, from the raw chemicals, but have disovered that there is no great advantage in doing so. Because of the quantities in which you have to buy the chemicals, you need to make up a lot of bleach-etch solution before you start to save any money.

▲ *Bleach-etching*

Make a print on RC paper and develop it in the usual way, but do not fix it. Rinse briefly, and transfer to the bleach-etch bath. This softens the exposed emulsion, which can then be rubbed off using a ball of cotton wool, as shown – wear rubber gloves!

▶ *Original image*

This straight print is all right, but a bit dull and ordinary. At first, bleach-etching is a way of spicing up such pictures, but after a while you start shooting certain subjects with bleach etch in mind. Complex, ornate shapes, with plenty of detail, often work well.

► *Pseudo-solarization*

Abraded under safelight, washed for two minutes, then redeveloped, fixed and washed. Pseudo-solarization, and what are called 'Mackie lines' around the light/dark boundaries, are the result.

▼ *Black-white reversal*

Abraded under room light, washed for two minutes, then redeveloped, fixed and washed. All the areas that were formerly white are now black.

- In bleach-etching, the print can be returned several times to the bath if you want to soften it some more. Whether you work under normal room light or safelight, and what you do to the print afterwards, affects the final image.

- A light touch is essential. Many gentle strokes give more control than a few brisk ones. Practise on scrap prints first.

- 'Surgical' rubber gloves are thin enough to let you feel changes in the surface texture.

▼ *White on white*

Abraded under room light, washed for two minutes, then fixed and washed. The result is 'white on white', but the areas where the gelatine has not been removed will accept dyes, as here.

COMPUTER MANIPULATION

Computer manipulation can arouse strong feelings in aficionados of the traditional 'wet' darkroom, but there is no doubt that some effects can be achieved much more easily, much more controllably, and often better, by using a computer program such as Adobe Photoshop — the four images on the opposite page were manipulated and created using various controls in Photoshop.

Although it is at first fascinating to see what you can do with the various filters, the 'Curvers' and 'Brightness/Contrast' controls and so forth, remember that a lot of the effects that you can create are now so easy that they have lost their impact and become clichés.

Always ask yourself why you are applying a particular effect. Even if it passes the test of 'Because it looks good', rather than 'Because I can', t may still end up looking hackneyed.

On the other hand, it is entirely true that many pictures that are intrinsically dull, flawed or uninteresting in conventional form can be saved — even transformed — by computer manipulation, and that even a picture that is completely useless on its own can be raided for components for a more complex 'comped' or assembled image.

◀ *Lith effect*

'Lith' means two things in photography: the process described on page 112, and a process by which very-high contrast (essentially pure black and pure white) was achieved by the use of high-contrast materials and developers. Today, ultra-high contrast is easier to achieve, with better results, via the 'contrast' and 'brightness' controls in Adobe Photoshop, or with other image-manipulation programs.

◀ *Posterization effect*

Posterization is another process which used to be done in the 'wet' darkroom, making two (or more) enlarged negatives on lith film and then contact-printing them in register. Today, it is quicker and easier to do it electronically: this was done using 'Posterize' in Adobe Photoshop.

▲ *Pseudo-solarization effect*

Pseudo-solarization (actually, the Sabbatier effect) was traditionally achieved by exposing a developing negative to light, about two minutes into the development; finishing development; and then contact-printing onto a high-contrast paper or film. Once again, the effect is much more easily obtained today via an image-manipulation program: this was done via 'Curves' in Adobe Photoshop.

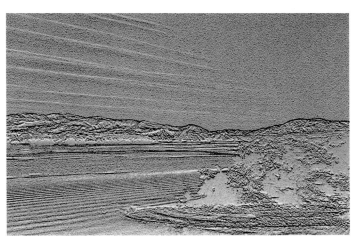

▲ *Bas-relief effect*

The traditional way to achieve a photographic bas-relief was by contact printing a negative onto film to make a corresponding positive; shifting the two slightly out of register; and then printing the sandwiched pair. The result looked like a low-relief carving in stone. Yet again, a substantially identical effect is achievable more easily via a single Adobe Photoshop filter, called (appropriately enough) 'Bas relief'.

GLOSSARY

Several of the entries in this list do not appear anywhere else in the book. They are included here so that you will be able to understand them better if you come across them in other books, or in the advice you are given by other photographers.

Acetic acid. A weak acid, normally used strongly diluted in Short stop. The main ingredient of vinegar.

Acutance. A measure of sharpness. High-acutance developers deliver more sharpness, though often with coarser grain.

Anti-foggant. A chemical added to developer to prevent Fog. Often known as a restrainer. Typically potassium bromide or benzotriazole.

Archival processing. Processing for maximum life. Involves thorough Washing and (often) Toning.

Archival storage. Storage under optimum conditions for long print (or negative) life: low temperatures, moderate humidity and an absence of contaminants such as are found in poor-quality boxes or mounting boards or negative sleeves.

Baryta. 'Baryt' in German, the whitening agent used to get the bright-white background of FB (fibre-based) papers.

Benzotriazole. See Anti-foggant.

Bleaching. Local or overall reduction of the silver image in a print or negative.

Blocked up. Shadows (in a print) or Highlights (in a negative) that are a solid, featureless black, without detail or texture.

Blown. A common description of Highlights (in a print) that are a featureless white, without any texture or detail.

Bright. An old euphemism (like Plucky) for negatives with a higher-than-average contrast.

Bromide. To a chemist, a salt of hydrobromic acid. In photography, normally silver bromide, AgBr. 'Bromide' is also used as a synonym for 'black-and-white print'.

Bromoil. A 'control process' in which a pigmented ink is used to build up an image in proportion to the (bleached-out) silver image.

Burned out. Similar to 'Blown'.

Burning. Giving extra exposure in localized areas of the print, to capture detail recorded on the negative which would otherwise print too light.

C-41. Kodak's proprietary name for the standard process for colour-negative film, which can also be used with Chromogenic films.

Changing bag. A light-tight bag for loading developing tanks, etc.

Chemistry. A term for the various chemical baths used to process films and papers.

Chromogenic films. Black-and-white films, such as Ilford XP2 Super, that can be developed in standard C-41 colour-film Chemistry.

Citric acid. A weak acid normally used in odourless Short stop.

Clearing time. The time it takes to remove the visible Silver halide from a film.

Combination print. A print made from more than one negative.

Contact print. A print made by sandwiching together a negative and a piece of paper; a print made without an enlarger.

Contact sheet. A sheet of images produced by making a Contact print of a whole 35mm film or roll film.

Contrast index or CI. A refinement of Gamma. A high CI or gamma means more contrast; a low CI or gamma means less contrast. Most negatives are developed to a CI of 0.55–0.70, depending on subject matter, the type of enlarger in use, and the preferences of the photographer.

Cool tone. Papers or developers that tend to produce bluish-backs.

Cropping. 'Throwing away' part of the image area recorded on the negative.

Developer. A chemical bath that 'brings up' the Latent image on exposed film.

Developing agent. The active ingredient in a Developer. Many developers have two (or more) developing agents, which are more effective in combination than you would expect from the activity of either on its own. This is called 'superadditivity'.

Developing-out. A paper which is developed, as distinct from Printing-out paper. All modern papers are developed-out.

Dodging. Holding back exposure in localized areas of the print, to capture detail recorded on the negative which would otherwise print too dark.

Dry-down. The loss of contrast and 'sparkle' in a print, and the increase in density, as it dries.

Dry-mounting. Mounting using a hot press and a fusible tissue.

Dry side. The side of the darkroom where dry work such as film loading, film-tank loading, paper cutting and enlarging are carried out. Kept separate from the wet side.

Emulsion. A suspension of Silver halide in gelatine: the light-sensitive part of a film or paper.

FB. Abbreviation for 'fibre-based' (or 'fiber-base') printing papers, without any plastic coating.

Finishing. The old term for Spotting.

Fixer. A chemical bath that dissolves out the unexposed Silver halide in a print or negative.

Flat. Lacking in contrast; without good blacks and pure white; muddy.

Flush-mounting. A way of mounting a print so that it is level with the board on which it is mounted, via spray adhesives or Dry-mounting.

Fog. Unexposed Silver halide will develop to a limited extent, leading to an overall grey veil or mask over the negative or print. Unsuitable developers can lead to fog; so can over age materials. In both cases, an Anti-foggant can reduce fog levels, though normally at the expense of reducing Speed.

G or 'G-bar'. Very similar to Contrast index.

Gamma. A measure of contrast in negatives; an older, cruder version of Contrast index.

Glazing. Imparting a high gloss to FB papers.

Glycin. A Developing agent used in Warm-tone developers.

Grade. A measure of the contrast of a paper. The lower the number, the lower the contrast. See ISO (R).

Graduate. A measuring jug or cylinder.

Hardening fixer. A Fixer that hardens the film or print during fixing. Greatly increases washing times. Rarely, if ever, needed today.

Highlights. The light areas of a print, or the dark areas of a negative.

Hydroquinone. An important, high-contrast developing agent, normally used in conjunction with Metol or Phenidone. Often called 'Quinol'.

Hypo. Old (and inaccurate) name for sodium thiosulphate, the basis of most types of Fixer.

Inertia. All Silver-halide materials have a 'threshold' below which an exposure is too weak to record. Only exposures which overcome this 'inertia' will record an image. Pre-flashing is used to overcome inertia.

Intensifier. A chemical bath that increases the density of an under-exposed or under-developed negative. Delivers terrible quality with most modern materials.

ISO (R). A measure of the contrast or Grade of a paper. Papers with higher ISO (R) numbers are 'softer' or exhibit less contrast and are suitable for contrasty negatives: papers with lower ISO (R) numbers are 'harder' or exhibit more contrast and are suitable for Flat negatives. Unfortunately, this is the opposite way around from paper grades: low-grade numbers imply a high ISO (R), while high-grade numbers imply a low ISO(R).

Kodalk. A proprietary alkali used in some Developers.

Lamp. Old slang term for an enlarger.

Landscape. In addition to the obvious meaning, a rectangular picture that is wider than it is high.

Latent image. An image on film or paper, after exposure but before development.

Liquid emulsion. Silver-halide emulsion in jellied form. Can be liquefied (by gentle heating) and applied to any number of surfaces.

Lith. Either a very high-contrast image, or an image that is incompletely developed in weak, partially exhausted developer to create special effects.

Metol. A widely used low-contrast Developing agent.

MQ. Abbreviation for Metol-Quinol developer.

Multigrade. Ilford trade-mark for variable-contrast (VC) paper, which they invented.

PE. Abbreviation for 'polyethylene', the resin used in RC papers. Used by some manufacturers (especially German) to indicate RC.

Phenidone. A widely used low-contrast Developing agent. It is often used to replace Metol, as it is more active and less likely to cause dermatitis.

Pin line. A thin black line around the image area on a print.

Plucky. An old euphemism (like Bright) for negatives with a higher-than-average contrast.

PMK (Pyro-Metol-Kodalk). A Staining developer for which impressive claims are made: photographers tend either to be believers or non-believers.

Portrait. In addition to the obvious meaning, a rectangular picture that is higher than it is wide.

Post-flashing. Similar to Pre-flashing, but after the exposure. Of disputable value.

PQ. Abbreviation for Phenidone-Quinol developer.

Pre-flashing. Giving a short pre-exposure to overcome the Inertia of printing paper, to get better Highlight detail.

Printing-out or POP. Paper that is not developed, but 'prints out' a visible image as a result of exposure to light. Very slow, and therefore suitable only for making Contact prints, normally by sunlight.

Pushing. Increasing development to compensate for under-exposure. There will be some loss of shadow detail, but this may not matter.

Pyro, pyrogallol, pyrogallic acid. A fairly toxic Developing agent.

Pyrocatechin. A fine-grain Developing agent.

Quinol. An old name for Hydroquinone.

RC. 'Resin-coated', a polyethylene coating applied to photographic paper to make it easier to handle and quicker to process.

Reducer. A chemical bath that decreases the density of an over-exposed or overdeveloped negative. Delivers terrible quality with most modern materials.

Restrainer. See Anti-foggant.

Retouching. Handwork on a negative or print to remove faults or simply to make it look better, e.g. by removing wrinkles in a portrait, or lightening clouds in a landscape. Often used interchangeably (but not entirely accurately) with **Spotting**.

Safelight. A light which will not affect sensitive materials.

Sandwich. Printing two negatives in the same carrier at the same time.

Shadows. The dark areas of a print, or the light areas of a negative.

Short stop. A bath that arrests the operation of **Developer**: optional between developer and **Fixer**.

Silver halide. A silver salt with one of the halide group of elements, whether fluoride, chloride, bromide or iodide. Silver halides are decomposed by the action of light into metallic silver and the halide in question (fluorine, chlorine, bromine, iodine). Because this is the basis of the vast majority of modern **Wet** photography, often known as 'silver-halide photography'.

Sodium sulphide. A crystalline compound with a strong smell of rotten eggs, used to make up traditional sulphide **Toner**.

Sodium sulphite. An important ingredient in most **Developers**, as a preservative. It stops the **Developing agent**(s) from oxidizing. The anhydrous version may be substituted for the crystalline, at half the weight.

Sodium thiosulphate. A long-established **Fixer**. Normally encountered in crystalline form: in the anhydrous form, only about 60 per cent of the weight required in crystalline form is needed to create the same strength solutions.

Soup. A long-obsolete slang term for **Developer**, still occasionally encountered in the United States.

Speed. Sensitivity. 'Fast' films and papers require less exposure than 'slow' ones.

Spotting. Removing white or (more rarely) black spots on a negative or print, the results of dust or imperfect processing.

Staining developer. A developer which stains the gelatine **Emulsion** in direct proportion to the degree of development. The stain is normally yellow, which is fine with graded papers, but can wreak havoc with VC papers.

Superadditivity. See Developing agent.

Test strip. A small print, usually of a part of the image area, made to check the optimum exposure time and contrast for a **Work print**.

Thiourea. The normal active ingredient in 'odourless' sepia **Toner**.

Toner. A chemical bath that changes the colour of the silver image. Also used of 'toners' that improve **Archival processing**, whether or not they change the image colour.

Universal developer. A Developer that can be used (normally at different dilutions) for both negatives and prints. Rarely very good for either.

Variable-contrast (VC). Papers that allow different contrast levels to be obtained, according to the colour of the light used to print the negative.

Warm tone. Papers or developers that tend to produce brownish-blacks.

Wash aid. A chemical bath used to speed Washing.

Washing. One of the most important steps in Wet processing, removing unwanted chemicals from the processed negative or print. Under-washing will result in staining and fading, but there is no need to wash for longer than the times recommended in this book: additional washing will do no good, and only wastes water. For washing with very cold water, below 10°C (40°F), some authorities recommend doubling wash times: others reckon it makes no difference.

Wet processing. Silver-halide photography, in contradistinction to digital or electronic or solid-state image capture, and ink-jet or similar image-output devices.

Wet side. The side of the darkroom where wet work, such as film and paper processing, toning and washing, is carried out.

Wetting agent. A chemical that reduces the surface tension of the water, allowing it to run off more easily and thereby reducing the risk of drying marks.

Window mount. A mount, usually of cardboard, with a cut-out in it, through which the print is seen as if through a window.

Work print. An early print, made to see what the negative will print like without any further manipulation.

WEIGHTS AND MEASURES AND FILTRATION FOR PAPER GRADES

The metric system is now all but universal in scientific and technical work, and when making up solutions it is easiest simply to work in that system without trying to translate back into earlier systems of weights and measures.

The only real exception to this is linear measure, in which (by ancient tradition) many film and paper sizes are expressed. Changing to round, metric numbers would mean changing film holders and many other pieces of equipment, so the old imperial sizes remain. The most usual standard film and paper sizes, in both imperial and metric, are given in the panel on page 125.

The tables and conversions here are principally for use when comparing old formulae with modern ones, though older readers may find them a useful reminder. The only real holdout against the metric system is the United States.

An important point is that the imperial (British) system, formerly used throughout the Empire, is not the same as the American system, used almost exclusively in the United States. Although the measures for weight are effectively identical, the American pint, quart and gallon are just over four-fifths of the size of their British equivalents and it is very important to know which system you are dealing with.

To make life still more confusing, imperial and American fluid ounces are also slightly different in size (the American fluid ounce is about four per cent bigger than imperial). This is unlikely to matter in most formulations, but it cannot be ignored if the utmost accuracy is sought.

The units of weight are also rendered all the more confusing because there is a choice between apothecary measure (abbreviated 'ap'), and the more common avoirdupois (abbreviated 'av'), which is the same as the normal American system. Again, it is essential to know which you are using.

When mixing chemicals where measures are given in both imperial and metric (or American and metric), it is normally essential to stick with one set of figures or the other, as the conversions are seldom exact. Typically, for example, the final volume will be one litre; or one imperial quart (40 fl oz); or one American quart (32 fl oz); and all other quantities will have been adjusted to reflect those final volumes.

In order to avoid an absolutely ridiculous range of conversion factors, only the more obvious and basic factors are given below; anyone with a calculator (and enough patience) can work out the conversion factor for grains per imperial fluid ounce to ounces per US pint to grams per litre.

Only units normally relevant to darkroom work have been given here: tons/tonnes, miles, kilometres, etc., have therefore been omitted.

THE METRIC SYSTEM

The basic unit of weight is the gram, which is linked to the basic unit of volume (the litre) and the basic unit of linear measurement (the metre).

One gram is the weight of one cubic centimetre (cc) or millilitre (ml) of water at 20°C (68°F).

1000 milligrams (mg) = 1 gram (g)
1000 grams (g) = 1 kilogram (Kg)

1000 millilitres (ml) = 1 litre (l)

1000 millimetres = 1 metre
100 centimetres = 1 metre

Imperial linear measure
12 inches = 1 foot
3 feet = 1 yard

Imperial volumetric measure
60 minims = 1 fluid drachm
8 fluid drachms = 1 fluid ounce (fl oz)
20 fluid ounces = 1 pint
2 pints = 1 quart (40 fl oz)
4 quarts (8 pints) = 1 gallon (160 fl oz)

American volumetric measure
60 minims = 1 fluid drachm
8 fluid drachms = 1 fluid ounce
16 fluid ounces = 1 pint
2 pints = 1 quart (32 fl oz)
4 quarts (8 pints) = 1 gallon (128 fl oz)

Avoirdupois weights
437.5 grains = 1 ounce (oz)
16 ounces (7000 grains) = 1 pound (lb)

Apothecaries' weight

20 grains = 1 scruple

3 scruples = 1 drachm

8 drachms (480 grains) = 1 ounce

12 ounces = 1 pound

Conversion factors – weight

1 grain = 0.065 gram

1 scruple = 1.30 gram

1 drachm = 3.89 gram

1 ounce (av) = 28.3 gram

1 ounce (ap) = 31.1 gram

1 pound (ap) = 373.2 gram

1 pound (av) = 452.8 gram

Conversion factors – volume

1 minim (imp) = 0.059 ml

1 minim (US) = 0.062 ml

1 fluid drachm (imp) = 3.55 ml

1 fluid drachm (US) = 3.70 ml

1 fluid ounce (imp) = 28.4 ml

1 fluid ounce (US) = 29.6 ml

1 pint (US) = 473 ml

1 pint (imp) = 568 ml

Conversion factors – linear measure

1 inch = 2.54 cm

1 foot = 30.5 cm

1 yard = 91.5 cm

Cut film and paper sizes

Quarter plate = $3\frac{1}{4}$ x $4\frac{1}{4}$ in = 8.3 x 10.8 cm

Post card = $3\frac{1}{2}$ x $5\frac{1}{2}$ in = 8.9 x 13.3 cm

4 x 5 in = 10.2 x 12.7 cm

Half plate = $4\frac{3}{4}$ x $6\frac{1}{2}$ in = 12.1 x 16.5 cm

5 x 7 in = 12.7 x 17.8 cm

8 x 10 in = 20.3 x 25.4 cm (often rendered as 20 x 25)

10 x 12 in = 25.4 x 30.5 cm

11 x 14 in = 28 x 35.6 cm

12 x 16 in = 30.5 x 40.6 cm (often rendered as 30 x 40)

16 x 20 in = 40.6 x 50.8 cm (often rendered as 40 x 50)

20 x 24 in = 50.8 x 61 cm (often rendered as 50 x 60)

9 x 12 cm = 3.54 x 4.72 in

13 x 18 cm = 5.12 x 7.09 in

18 x 24 cm = 7.09 x 9.45 in

24 x 30 cm = 9.45 x 11.81 in

Larger sizes are close enough to imperial: see above

TEMPERATURES

The Celsius or Centigrade system is used almost everywhere in the world, with the exception of the United States. Water freezes at 0°C (32°F), and boils at 100°C (212°F).

The conversion factors are complicated by the differences in freezing point. To convert the temperature in degrees F to degrees C, subtract 32 then multiply by $\frac{5}{9}$ (0.56). To convert the temperature in degrees C to degrees F, multiply by $\frac{9}{5}$ (1.8) and then add 32.

The standard temperature for development for most of the first half of the 20th century was 18°C (65°F), after which it rose to 20°C (68°F). Today, times are normally given for 20°C (68°F), or 21°F (70°C), or 24°C (75°F). Obviously, you need to know which is recommended for a particular developer.

PERCENTAGE SOLUTIONS

A percentage solution is normally specified as w/v (weight-per-volume) or v/v (volume-per-volume). Thus, a 10 per cent solution w/v of hypo is 100 gm of hypo in 1000 ml of water, while a 0.5 per cent solution of wetting agent is 0.5 ml in 1000 ml.

Colour-head settings for paper-contrast grades

The table below, courtesy of Ilford, gives the magenta and yellow settings on colour heads for the various contrast grades for Ilford Multigrade paper, at constant exposure times. Several versions of this table exist, and not all agree. It is extremely advisable to check the current manufacturer's spec sheet for whatever paper you are using: most give the appropriate filtration values for their own paper. As far as we have been able to discover, the Durst family includes Dunco, Kaiser, Kienzle, current Paterson, Leitz and Lupo, but some have 170M maximum filtration, while others have 130M maximum, noted as Durst 170 and Durst 130. The Kodak family includes Advena, Beseler, Chromega, De Vere, Fujimoto, IFF, Jobo, LPL, Omega, old Paterson, Simmard and Vivitar. Meopta and Krokus require similar filtration to Kodak for grades 0 to 2, but increasing amounts of magenta thereafter: the maximum contrast obtainable is grade $4\frac{1}{2}$ at 0Y/200M.

Grade	Durst 170	Durst 130	Kodak
00	115Y/0M	120Y/0M	162Y/0M
0	100Y/5M	88Y/6M	90Y/0M
$\frac{1}{2}$	88Y/7M	78Y/8M	78Y/5M
1	75Y/10M	64Y/12M	68Y/10M
$1\frac{1}{2}$	65Y/15M	53Y/17M	47Y/23M
2	52Y/20M	45Y/24M	41Y/32M
$2\frac{1}{2}$	42Y/28M	35Y/31M	32Y/42M
3	34Y/45M	24Y/42M	23Y/56M
$3\frac{1}{2}$	27Y/60M	17Y/53M	15Y/75M
4	17Y/76M	10Y/69M	6Y/102M
$4\frac{1}{2}$	10Y/105M	6Y/89M	0Y/150M
5	0Y/170M	0Y/130M	Not possible

INDEX

acknowledgements

Fairly clearly, a lot of the materials and equipment in this book came from Paterson, and we would like to thank Roger Parry for help in this and other projects, as well as for being a true enthusiast. The film and paper we used was almost exclusively Ilford: we use very little else, apart from Paterson, which is not available as widely as Ilford. At Ilford, we would like to thank Ian Callow for the materials, and Mike Gristwood and Tony Johnson for endless advice over the years.

We have also used (in alphabetical order) Alpa roll-film cameras from Alpa Capaul & Weber in Switzerland; Contax 35mm cameras from Kyocera UK; Gandolfi large-format cameras from Gandolfi Ltd; and Voigtlander 35mm cameras from Prisma UK Ltd. You can get excellent results with many other cameras, but you will always get the best results with cameras that you are happiest with, regardless of cost, and we have been very happy with all of the above. Among enlargers, we also use (and can recommend) Meopta cameras from RK Photographic in the UK and De Vere enlargers and heads from Odyssey Sales in the UK. The vast majority of our prints are developed in Nova tanks, washed in Nova deep-slot washers, and dried in a Nova RC paper drier; enlarger and process timing is by a mixture of RH Designs, Colorstar, and Nova.

For the use of prints, we would like to thank Dr Tim Rudman and Martin Reed. We can heartily recommend their books:

Spirits of Salts, a Working Guide to Old Photographic Processes, Randall Webb & Martin Reed, Argentum, 1999
The Photographer's Master Lith Printing Course, Tim Rudman, Argentum, 1998

Finally, we would like to thank all the authors of all the other books on photography that we have read over the decades — well, most of them, anyway — and all the photographers who have been willing to share their enthusiasm and knowledge with us. In particular, we would like to put on record the debt we owe to two friends who died, within a few weeks of one another, while this book was being written: Jack Cull, to whom the book is dedicated, and Colin Glanfield, who taught us more than we can say.